DEPRESSION

Questions
you
have
. . . Answers
you
need

Other Books From The People's Medical Society

Take This Book to the Hospital With You

How to Evaluate and Select a Nursing Home

Medicine on Trial

Medicare Made Easy

Your Medical Rights

Getting the Most for Your Medical Dollar

Take This Book to the Gynecologist With You

Take This Book to the Obstetrician With You

Blood Pressure: Questions You Have . . . Answers You Need

Your Heart: Questions You Have . . . Answers You Need

The Consumer's Guide to Medical Lingo

150 Ways to Be a Savvy Medical Consumer

Take This Book to the Pediatrician With You

100 Ways to Live to 100

Dial 800 for Health

Your Complete Medical Record

Arthritis: Questions You Have . . . Answers You Need

Diabetes: Questions You Have . . . Answers You Need

Prostate: Questions You Have . . . Answers You Need

Vitamins and Minerals: Questions You Have . . . Answers You Need

Good Operations—Bad Operations

The Complete Book of Relaxation Techniques

Test Yourself for Maximum Health

Misdiagnosis: Woman As a Disease

Yoga Made Easy

Hearing Loss: Questions You Have . . . Answers You Need

Asthma: Questions You Have . . . Answers You Need

DEPRESSION

Questions
you
have
...Answers
you
need

By Sandra Salmans

≡People's Medical Society®

Allentown, Pennsylvania

The People's Medical Society is a nonprofit consumer health organization dedicated to the principles of better, more responsive and less expensive medical care. Organized in 1983, the People's Medical Society puts previously unavailable medical information into the hands of consumers so that they can make informed decisions about their own health care.

Membership in the People's Medical Society is $20 a year and includes a subscription to the *People's Medical Society Newsletter.* For information, write to the People's Medical Society, 462 Walnut Street, Allentown, PA 18102, or call 610-770-1670.

This and other People's Medical Society publications are available for quantity purchase at discount. Contact the People's Medical Society for details.

© 1995 by the People's Medical Society
Printed in the United States of America

Library of Congress Cataloging-in-Publication Data
Salmans, Sandra.
    Depression : questions you have, answers you need /
by Sandra Salmans.
      p. cm.
    Includes bibliographical references and index.
    ISBN 1-882606-14-0
    1. Depression, Mental—Miscellanea.   2. Depression,
Mental—Popular works. I. Title.
RC537.S34 1995
616.85'27—dc20   94-39327
                                             CIP

1 2 3 4 5 6 7 8 9 0
First printing, December 1994

INTRODUCTION

There is certainly a lot of bad news associated with depression.

It has been called the "common cold of mental illness." Fifteen million Americans suffer from it each year. About half of its victims either do not know they have a depressive illness or have been misdiagnosed (by a medical professional) as suffering another malady.

Depression is growing in America and throughout the world. People born since World War II have a much higher incidence than those born earlier. But even older Americans have witnessed an increase in cases.

Depression is a nondiscriminating condition. It affects every age and race, and both sexes.

Depression is not a simple illness. There are many different depressive disorders, some not even displaying what we commonly think of as depressive symptoms. And depression often recurs after having been successfully treated on an earlier occasion.

Depression brings with it many problems. Aside from the medical and coping woes so common with the disorder, people with depressive conditions have often found themselves discriminated against on the job, socially excluded and even shunned by their own family. Sometimes the ostracism associated with depression has driven people with treatable conditions into isolation or institutions, or to their deaths.

But there is good news about depression as well. The good news is that most forms of depression are treatable. And even better news is that *successful* treatment is growing substantially each year. New medications, better interventions and the movement that is bringing depression "out of the closet" all are contributing to making depression less the onerous burden it once was.

Great progress is being made in understanding and treating depression. Laws have been enacted that protect people coping with depression from losing their jobs or being denied treatment. Insurers and employers are taking more enlightened views of the many depressive disorders.

DEPRESSION: QUESTIONS YOU HAVE . . . ANSWERS YOU NEED covers all the important facts you need to know about depression. From the various types of depressive disorders to the latest in treatment, DEPRESSION: QUESTIONS YOU HAVE . . . ANSWERS YOU NEED faces all the issues head-on. And the entire book is presented in an easy-to-read, understandable, question-and-answer format.

DEPRESSION: QUESTIONS YOU HAVE . . . ANSWERS YOU NEED answers all your questions and even some you may never have considered. It will surely become an invaluable asset in your overall confrontation with depression.

As the nation's largest consumer-health advocacy organization, the People's Medical Society is dedicated to getting helpful information to the consumer. It is our philosophy that an informed consumer is an empowered one—a person capable of making the best health-care decisions in partnership with her health-care provider.

Thus, the more you know about depression and its treatment options, the more likely you will be to find useful and significant help.

Charles B. Inlander
President
People's Medical Society

DEPRESSION

**Questions
you
have
... Answers
you
need**

Terms printed in boldface can be found in the glossary, beginning on page 169. Only the first mention of the word in the text will be boldfaced.

We have tried to use male and female pronouns in an egalitarian manner throughout the book. Any imbalance in usage has been in the interest of readability.

1 GETTING DOWN TO DEPRESSION

Q: What is **depression**?

A: It might be better to say immediately what depression is *not*. It's not just feeling temporarily "blue" or "down in the dumps" around the holidays, for example. It's more than being sad or feeling intense grief after the loss of a loved one. Sadness and grief are normal and temporary reactions to life's stresses. In psychotherapy, they're known as **adjustment disorders**. In days or weeks, people's moods lift, and they function normally again.

In contrast, depression—often referred to as **clinical depression**, **mood disorder** or **affective disorder**—affects people for months or even years. Depressive illnesses affect feelings, thoughts, behavior and physical well-being.

Q: But how serious is depression, really?

A: Health-care professionals describe depression as a disorder requiring intervention and treatment, just as any physical illness would. A much-cited Medical Outcomes Study, published in the *Journal of the American Medical Association* in 1989, reported that clinical depression is the

11

most incapacitating of all chronic conditions, in terms of
social functioning. It ranks second only to advanced heart
disease in exacting a physical toll, measured by days in bed
and body pain.

"Major depression is far more disabling than many medical disorders, including chronic lung disease, arthritis and
diabetes," says Frederick Goodwin, M.D., former director of
the National Institute of Mental Health (NIMH).

Measured another way, the annual cost of depression in
the United States was $43.7 billion in 1990, according to a
study published in the *Journal of Clinical Psychiatry.* That
sum represents a total of the cost of 290 million days lost
from work, poor performance on the job, psychotherapeutic
care and the loss of lifetime earnings due to suicide.

Q: How can I tell if I'm depressed?

A: A depression is a **syndrome**, or a constellation of
signs and symptoms. To diagnose it, most clinicians
use the criteria listed in the *Diagnostic and Statistical
Manual of Mental Disorders (DSM-IV)* of the American
Psychiatric Association. Those criteria are:

1. Depressed mood (sometimes irritability in children
and adolescents) most of the day, nearly every day.

2. Markedly diminished interest or pleasure in all, or
almost all, activities most of the day, nearly every day (as
indicated either by subjective account or observation by
others of apathy most of the time).

3. Significant weight loss or gain when not dieting
(more than 5 percent of body weight in a month), or decrease/
increase in appetite nearly every day. (In a child, this is
measured in terms of failure to meet expected weight gains.)

4. Insomnia or **hypersomnia** nearly every day.

5. **Psychomotor agitation** or **psychomotor retardation**—an abnormal speeding up or slowing down of one's
activities and mental processes—nearly every day, as observed

by others (not merely subjective feelings of restlessness or being slowed down).

6. Fatigue or loss of energy nearly every day.

7. Feelings of worthlessness or excessive or inappropriate guilt (which may be delusional) nearly every day (not merely self-reproach or guilt about being sick).

8. Diminished ability to think or concentrate, or indecisiveness, nearly every day.

9. Recurrent thoughts of death (not just fear of dying) or of suicide without a specific plan, or a suicide attempt or specific plan for committing suicide.

Q: **Do I have to have all these symptoms to be considered depressed?**

A: To qualify as a **major depressive disorder**, at least five of the symptoms must be present during the same two-week period. In addition, at least the first or second symptom must be present. And the condition cannot be a normal reaction to the recent death of a loved one.

Not everyone who's depressed experiences every symptom. Some people experience a few symptoms, some many. Also, the severity of symptoms varies with individuals and the kinds of depression that they're suffering.

Q: **The list reminds me of some questionnaires I've filled out at my doctor's office. Is it the same list?**

A: You may well have completed a form designed to uncover symptoms of depression, while you were waiting to see the doctor. In fact, there are four so-called self-report scales that are widely used by primary-care physicians to detect depression.

They are the General Health Questionnaire (GHQ), the Center for Epidemiological Studies—Depression Scale (CES-D), the Beck Depression Inventory (BDI) and the Zung Self-Rating Depression Scale (ZSRDS). For children between the ages of 8 and 17, there's a modification of the BDI called the Children's Depression Inventory.

Q: **How accurate are these scales?**

A: They detect nearly everyone who has a major depressive disorder, but frequently they also diagnose depression where it doesn't exist. In other words, for every one person they correctly diagnose with depression, the scales also say two to three people are depressed when they really aren't.

Q: **Diagnosing depression seems awfully inexact. Isn't there anything more scientific?**

A: There are laboratory tests, but their main purpose is to rule out potential medical causes for depression. We discuss those causes in Chapter 2.

Q: **So if I tell my doctor that I'm depressed, he'd give me a blood test?**

A: First he would probably want to spend more time talking with you and possibly with your family and/or friends, to develop a complete medical and psychiatric history. Your doctor might also administer a mental-status examination, which evaluates your level of motor activity and checks your speech and thought patterns and memory, which are often affected by mood disorders.

Only if there are other symptoms distinct from those of depression—for example, evidence of **dementia**—would the physician order neuropsychological or neurologic laboratory tests, such as an **electroencephalogram (EEG)** or **magnetic resonance imaging (MRI)**. Or if you meet certain other criteria—if, for example, you're a woman over 50 having your first depressive episode—you might be tested for thyroid function, since **hypothyroidism** occurs as frequently in this group as depression does and produces some of the same symptoms.

Q: Then there's no definitive test for depression?

A: So far, unfortunately, there are no definitive hormonal or blood tests to diagnose depression or predict response to a given treatment. Someday, however, sleep electroencephalograms may be used to detect depression.

Q: Sleep EEGs! What would they show?

A: Studies have shown that individuals with either **unipolar** or **bipolar** depression have sleep patterns different from those of people who do not have mood disorders. The rapid-eye-movement (REM) phase of sleep associated with dreaming occurs earlier in people with mood disorders. People with mood disorders also have more eye movements during REM sleep, less deep or slow-wave sleep, and more problems staying asleep.

Still, this pattern is most pronounced in people who are severely ill; it's not a reliable measure of less severe depression.

Q: It sounds like it's easy to misdiagnose depression. Am I right?

A: You're right, on two counts: Many cases of depression are mistakenly diagnosed by primary-care physicians as medical ailments, and many medical problems are misdiagnosed—particularly by psychiatrists—as depression. In fact, the false assumption of psychological illness has been described as "probably the most common error made in medicine."

In Chapter 2, we discuss a number of medical disorders and medications that can generate the symptoms of depression and lead to misdiagnoses.

Q: How frequently is depression overlooked?

A: A 1989 study by Rand, a research institution in Santa Monica, California, found that doctors who are not specialists in mental health miss the diagnosis of severe depression at least half the time. In an effort to improve those statistics, the U.S. Department of Health and Human Services assembled a Depression Guideline Panel of mental-health-care experts and others to create guidelines for general practitioners to use in diagnosing and treating depression. It's hoped that the guidelines, issued in 1993, can improve the diagnosis and treatment of depression.

Q: Why exactly does depression get misdiagnosed as a medical problem?

A: While some people who are deeply depressed often recognize their problems and want intervention, many others don't recognize the symptoms and are misled by what are known as **psychosomatic** problems: pains that are real but disappear when the depression is eliminated. Since the depression is "masked" by complaints of medical problems, primary-care physicians often make a medical diagnosis.

The diagnosis may be complicated by the fact that a great many individuals prefer to be diagnosed with a physical rather than a mental illness. This is particularly true among certain minority groups in the United States, notably Hispanics. Unfortunately, there's still a stigma attached to mental illness, even an illness as widespread as depression. According to the NIMH, half of all Americans still view depression as a personal weakness or a character flaw.

Q: Are there certain psychosomatic problems characteristic of depression?

A: It's common for people with depressive disorders to complain to their physicians about recurring headaches, backaches, abdominal pain, chronic fatigue, insomnia or indigestion. It's been found that 70 to 90 percent of people who seek medical care for irritable-bowel syndrome—a very common gastrointestinal disorder characterized by loose and frequent stools—also have psychiatric problems, usually major depression.

It's easy for physicians to be misled by these symptoms. In a study published in 1986, a group of gastroenterologists found that physicians almost invariably overlooked depression as a possible root cause of bowel disorders, thus leading to unnecessary testing and surgery.

FORMS OF DEPRESSIVE ILLNESSES

Q: Are there different forms of depression apart from major depressive disorder?

A: There are a great many forms of depression and numerous terms to describe them, some of them overlapping. For example, clinical depression is used to characterize any depression where symptoms are severe and lasting enough to require treatment. The most common form of clinical depression is major depressive disorder.

There's also a more severe form of major depression known as **melancholic depression**. *DSM-IV* defines melancholic depression as a condition in which the individual has lost interest or pleasure in all, or almost all, activities, and doesn't improve—even temporarily—when something good happens. It's a state of complete **anhedonia**—the inability to experience pleasure. By contrast, most people with classic major depressive disorder are able to be cheered up and even become animated temporarily.

Q: Is melancholic depression the most serious type of major depression?

A: No, there's a condition known as **psychotic depression**, or depression with psychotic features, which carries a major risk of suicide. People with psychotic depression have delusions or hallucinations, usually consistent with their predominant sad mood. For example, a person may have the delusion that he's sinned in an unforgivable way. As many as 15 percent of people with major depressive disorders develop psychotic depression, according to the Depression Guideline Panel of the U.S. Department of Health and Human Services.

Q: Are there other kinds of depression?

A: There's an anomalous disorder known as **atypical depression**, which, despite its name, is not uncommon. It turns the typical symptoms of depression upside down. While people with typical depression sleep and eat less than normal, people with atypical depression tend to oversleep, overeat and gain weight rapidly—behavior that is described as **vegetative**.

According to Donald Klein, M.D., a psychiatrist at the Columbia University College of Physicians and Surgeons, New York City, and a leading authority on depression, atypical depression is chronic rather than periodic, and usually dates from adolescence. People with this condition may show little energy or interest in anything, and are extremely sensitive to rejection, particularly romantic rejection.

Q: You've been talking about "major" depressions. Are there "mild" depressions?

A: That's one way to characterize a disorder known as **dysthymia**, which used to be called neurotic depression. To meet the definition of dysthymia—literally, "ill-humored"—the depression has to have been present for at least two years. People with dysthymia don't have symptoms that are as severe as those for major depressive disorder, but they never feel really well.

In an interview in *American Health* magazine, psychologist James McCullough, Ph.D., director of the Unipolar Mood Disorders Institute at Virginia Commonwealth University, Richmond, Virginia, compared dysthymia to "a low-grade infection people just can't get rid of. They're not taken out of the work force or the home—they just feel bad most of the time."

Q: What are the characteristics of dysthymia?

A: In an article in the *American Journal of Psycho-therapy,* Hagop S. Akiskal, M.D., of the University of California at San Diego, wrote that people with dysthymia "invest whatever 'energy' they have in work, with none left for leisure and other family or social activities, hence the marital friction so characteristic of their colorless lives that appears to be one of overdedication to work." Other researchers have described a sense of "dutiful self-denial."

Martin B. Keller, M.D., of the Brown University School of Medicine in Providence, Rhode Island, has described dysthymia as "one of the most difficult psychiatric illnesses to diagnose and manage" because it's often accompanied by related psychiatric illnesses.

Q: Why isn't dysthymia considered just a basic personality trait?

A: In fact, historically people suffering from chronic depression were said to have depressive personalities or a **personality disorder**. In 1980, however, the American Psychiatric Association reclassified dysthymia as an affective disorder. Research by Akiskal and others placed dysthymia on one end of a spectrum, with major depressive disorder at the other, based on such factors as family history, the course of the illness and its response to medication.

Q: Do people with dysthymia ever develop more severe depressions?

A: Some studies have shown that the majority of people with dysthymia go on to develop major depression. When this happens, they're said to have **double depression**. Compared with typical major depressive disorder, double depression can be particularly serious and difficult to treat. And individuals who undergo double depression are at much higher risk for a recurrence.

Q: **Are there any other types of depression?**

A: At least two other forms, which are unique to women and appear to be related to hormone levels. A discussion of these appears in Chapter 2.

Q: **You haven't mentioned manic depression. What's the difference between that and the other conditions?**

A: The disorders we've just described are all forms of unipolar depression. Manic depression, or **manic-depressive disorder**, is a bipolar disorder, because it involves alternating episodes of serious mania and depression.

Q: **What exactly happens in manic depression?**

A: In their depressed phases, manic depressives exhibit the symptoms associated with major depression. When they're manic, their symptoms are almost diametrically opposite. People with manic depression are often described as being on an emotional roller coaster.

On average, the manic phase lasts one to three months, while the period of depression lasts six to nine months. They may be separated by periods of normal or near-normal functioning. However, some people with manic depression may exhibit a "rapid-cycling" pattern, in which they experience four or more mood episodes per year.

Q: What's a person like when he is manic?

A: A person in a manic phase will have some or all of the following symptoms:
- Increased energy
- Decreased need for sleep (The tapering-off of sleeping hours is often a sign that the manic phase is beginning.)
- Increased risk-taking
- Unrealistic beliefs in his own abilities and powers
- Increased talking and physical, social and sexual activity
- Extreme euphoria, irritability and distractibility
- Obnoxious, provocative or intrusive behavior
- Abuse of drugs, particularly cocaine, alcohol and sleeping medications.

Q: Aren't people who are manic depressive supposed to be especially creative?

A: It is true that a number of famous writers and artists —including Ernest Hemingway, Virginia Woolf and possibly Mark Twain—apparently had bipolar disorder. It's even been suggested that Beethoven, Vincent Van Gogh and Gustav Mahler may have been manic depressives.

In her book *Touched With Fire: Manic-Depressive Illness and the Artistic Temperament,* Johns Hopkins psychologist Kay Redfield Jamison estimated that rates of manic depression are several times higher among artists than in the general public.

"People with manic depression have faster, more fluid thinking, high energy levels and a wide range of emotional experience to draw on, from elation to despair," says Jamison. "Artists have to go where others won't, emotionally speaking, and manic depressives do that automatically."

Q: What's so bad about that?

A: Let's remember that, for all their bursts of creativity when they were manic, many of these people paid a high price when they fell back into the inevitable depression. Hemingway and Woolf, for example, both committed suicide.

And for most people, the manic phase is just plain destructive, costing them jobs, friends and family. Individuals, when manic, tend to overlook the painful or harmful consequences of their behavior. They may incur huge debts, make poor business decisions and be extremely promiscuous sexually. They may even break the law and land in jail.

Q: Does the mania ever really go dangerously out of control?

A: Some people in manic episodes do become psychotic. They may suffer delusions that fit the grandiosity of their moods—for example, hearing God telling them they have a special mission or special powers, or suffering delusions of persecution because of their unique attributes.

Q: Are there different forms of manic depression, too?

A: There's actually a lot of variation in the disorder, measured by the highs and lows and the periods in between. Some people with manic depression have repeated depressions and only occasional episodes of mania. Some have what's called "mixed mood disorder," in which they experience intense depression and mania at the same time. And a small percentage of people with bipolar disorder experience only manic episodes.

In **hypomania**, people experience severe depressions with relatively mild manic phases. There's also a condition called **cyclothymia**, marked by extremely short mood swings— days or weeks—between hypomania and mild depression. For cyclothymics—about 10 percent of all people with bipolar disorder—there are few truly symptom-free periods.

Q: Aren't there some people who get depressed only in winter?

A: Yes. Some people suffer from a condition known as **seasonal affective disorder (SAD)**, which usually begins in the fall and lifts dramatically in the spring. People with SAD report that their depressions worsen the farther north they live and the more overcast the weather. While SAD has been linked mainly to dark winter days, in some cases it's been associated with dark indoor work spaces, unseasonable cloudy spells and vision difficulties.

Some experts believe the high rate of alcoholism and suicide in northern countries such as Sweden may be due to SAD. Higher-than-average SAD rates have also been reported in New Hampshire and the upper Midwest, and very low rates in Florida.

Q: Doesn't everyone get the doldrums in winter?

A: SAD isn't the usual winter doldrums or cabin fever. For one thing, the average SAD episode lasts five months. Moreover, SAD symptoms include many of the usual features of depression, especially decreased sexual appetite, lethargy and social withdrawal.

Other symptoms are mixed. People with SAD may have either insomnia or hypersomnia so severe that they have trouble maintaining a normal 9-to-5 job. They may also have

a craving for carbohydrates and gain considerable weight
during this period. (The intensity of the symptoms varies
from the extreme to the mild, or subsyndromal SAD—S-SAD.)

INCIDENCE OF DEPRESSION

Q: How common is depression?

A: It has been called "the common cold of mental
illness" and, like the cold, it's difficult to quantify.
The Epidemiologic Catchment Area study indicates that, in
any given month, 2.2 percent of Americans will have a major
depressive order, and 5.8 percent will experience an episode
sometime during their lives. Put yet another way, according
to the National Institutes of Health (NIH), some 15 million
Americans will become seriously depressed in the course
of a year.

Other studies estimate lifetime prevalence to be much
higher—up to 26 percent for females and 12 percent for males.

Mood disorders, including depression, are also the most
common single reason for visits to psychiatrists' offices—
28 percent in 1989 and 1990, according to a survey by the
National Center for Health Statistics—and account for 70 percent of psychiatric hospitalizations.

Q: What about dysthymia?

A: It is estimated that dysthymia, which often begins in
childhood or adolescence, affects 3 to 4 percent of
Americans, most of them women. According to the NIMH,
between 20 and 30 percent of people who are diagnosed
with depression are actually dysthymic.

Q: And manic depression? How common is that?

A: According to the NIH, almost 2 million Americans suffer from manic-depressive illnesses each year. Typically they begin in adolescence or early adulthood— earlier than unipolar depression—and, untreated, continue throughout life, occurring more frequently and becoming more severe over time.

Unlike unipolar depression, bipolar depression afflicts men and women in equal numbers, although studies show that 80 to 90 percent of "rapid cyclers" are women.

Q: How common is SAD?

A: By one estimate, 5 percent of the U.S. population gets SAD. It's also been estimated that anywhere from 10 to 38 percent of those suffering from recurrent mood disorders actually have SAD.

Like major depression, SAD occurs more often in women. According to Norman E. Rosenthal, M.D., a psychiatrist with the NIMH who has studied SAD, women are three to four times more likely to suffer from SAD than men. It usually increases after puberty and subsides with menopause.

Q: Frankly, depression seems a little trendy. I don't remember hearing my grandparents talk about being depressed. Is this something new?

A: In fact, depression is a disease that can be traced back to antiquity. *The Book of Job,* for example, describes a loss of interest, social withdrawal, self-deprecation and insomnia. The ancient Romans called the condition *melancholia,* the Victorians knew it as *neurasthenia.*

And even if your grandparents didn't suffer from it or talk about it, one of their most famous contemporaries did: Winston Churchill, the British prime minister who guided his country through World War II, described the "black bear" that periodically cast him into gloom.

Q: **But depression seems to be much more in vogue these days, wouldn't you say?**

A: It is true that depression has soared with the coming of age of the baby boomers. Two major government-sponsored studies begun in the 1970s found a striking rise in the incidence of depression over the course of the century. The studies led Gerald Klerman, a prominent mental-health expert who was director of the umbrella agency over NIMH at that time, to call the era the "Age of Melancholy."

One study found that women born during the Korean War period—meaning that they were about 30 years old at the time of the study—were 20 times more likely to have had an episode of depression than women born around World War I, even though the older women had had much more time to become depressed. The same trend was true of men.

If you go back even farther, the contrast sharpens. Only 1 percent of Americans born before 1905 had suffered a major depression by age 75.

Q: **Is the increase in depression limited to the United States?**

A: No, not at all. Data gathered by the Cross-National Collaborative Group point to a real change in depression rates worldwide. For example, baby boomers in Florence, Italy, showed nearly double the rate of depression beginning at age 15, compared with compatriots born before World War II.

Q: Why is depression increasing?

A: It could be just that the spotlight is on it now, and it's being diagnosed and studied more intently. Other possible reasons that have been suggested include increased drug and alcohol use, rising stress levels and decreasing employment opportunities.

Another possible source for the increase in depression is fundamental societal change. According to Martin Seligman, a psychologist at the University of Pennsylvania, Philadelphia, our society has developed an unhealthy focus on "the self" and individuals are excessively concerned with their own gratifications and losses.

In the absence of a commitment to a larger good—to God, country or family, for instance—personal failures seem catastrophic. "Depression and meaninglessness follow from self-preoccupation," Seligman has written in a recent book, *Learned Optimism.*

Q: That's all theory, of course. Are there any studies pinpointing reasons for the growing prevalence of depression?

A: Some research suggests that television is a major source of depression. A recent study by Paul Kettl, M.D., a psychiatrist at Penn State University-Milton S. Hershey Medical Center, Hershey, Pennsylvania, found a high correlation between the presence of television in households when children were growing up and the onset of major depression by the age of 24.

"The social effects of television, broadcasting seven hours per day to the average American home, must be included as a possible reason for the earlier onset and growth of major depression among the young," Kettl writes. "Thousands of hours of TV viewing expose our children to repetitive acts of senseless violence and may further distance children from social contacts with peers and family.''

Q: What's the typical age for the onset of depression?

A: While major depressive disorder may begin at any age, it most commonly sets in among people in their 20s and 30s. Rates are highest for adults between the ages of 25 and 44.

Q: How long does an episode of depression last?

A: Even without any treatment, most depressed people get better within six months to a year. With treatment, people may recover far more quickly—within a matter of a few weeks or months. In the case of dysthymia, however, only about 10 to 15 percent of cases clear up on their own.

Q: What's the risk of recurrence?

A: It's quite high. According to a study published in the *Journal of Clinical Psychiatry* in 1991, more than half of all people who've had a major depressive disorder will have a recurrence, many within two to three years of their first episodes. The risk rises with the number of episodes, to 70 percent after two episodes and to 90 percent after three episodes.

Q: What, exactly, are the risk factors for recurrence?

A: You're at higher risk that depression will recur if:

- your first episode occurs at an early age—say, before 20—and there's a family history of the disorder. One study found that 72 percent of children who had a major depressive disorder had a second episode within five years.
- your initial episode was severe and you were relatively slow to respond to therapy
- you have other psychiatric and medical illnesses
- you're particularly vulnerable to stresses or other psychosocial factors. A recent study found that people's ability to manage stress, as well as their social relationships, can affect the rate of recurrence.
- you haven't recovered fully from your previous depression
- you developed depression late in life.

Q: Does that mean that depression can recur without any triggering cause?

A: According to Robert Post, a scientist at NIMH, once something has triggered an initial episode of depression, people are more vulnerable to additional episodes. The initial episode has a "kindling effect" that makes people more prone to recurrences. "While a psychosocial stress can be involved in the onset of the first episode, the trigger mechanism for subsequent depressions can be more autonomous," he says.

RISK GROUPS FOR DEPRESSION

Q: Who's most likely to develop depression?

A: As the statistics on incidence show, women are the primary risk group, diagnosed with depression at least twice as often as men.

Admittedly, there's some thinking that men become depressed just as often but that, because our society expects men to be tough-minded and stiff-upper-lipped, most have a hard time talking about emotional distress or showing weakness, and are likelier than women to "self-medicate" with alcohol or narcotics. Furthermore, according to the Hart Survey of Americans on Mental Illness and Depression, men are more likely than women to attach a social stigma to depression—and thus, seemingly, are less willing to admit they're depressed.

In fact, a much-cited study carried out in the 1980s found that men and women in the Amish community of Lancaster County, Pennsylvania, developed major mood disorders at a similar rate. Researchers noted that the Amish culture prohibits the use of alcohol and drugs—closing that particular escape route to men—and that, since crime is rare among the Amish, none of the men were lost to the study because they were in prison.

But the notion that men develop major depressive order as often as women is clearly a minority view. In Chapter 2 we discuss the possible reasons behind women's high rates of depression.

Q: What other groups are at risk for depression?

A: Not surprisingly, elderly people in institutions, whether long-term care or acute-care facilities, are often severely depressed. The NIMH says that between 10 and 20 percent have major depressive disorder; other sources double that estimate.

Q: What about elderly people who aren't institutionalized?

A: In general, their rate of clinical depression may actually be lower than that of younger people— perhaps only 1 to 2 percent, according to the NIH. In addition, another 10 percent, while technically not suffering from major depressive disorder, may have significant symptoms of depression.

Q: But, in general, elderly people are less depressed than the population overall?

A: Yes, you can make that generalization, but with a few provisos. For one thing, the high incidence of Alzheimer's disease and other age-related diseases means that depression in the elderly is often overlooked. A report by the NIH called depression in those over 65 "insidious" because, in many cases, neither the patient nor the health provider can distinguish depression from the person's other ailments.

An example is **pseudodementia**, a form of depression in which memory seems to fade, and complicated thinking and concentration become difficult. When pseudodementia occurs in the elderly, it is often misdiagnosed as Alzheimer's or senile dementia.

There's also evidence that the elderly themselves under-report depressive symptoms. That's partly because they expect to be depressed at their age and, unlike their more psychologically oriented offspring, believe they should be stoic. "The elderly tend to consider depression to be a symptom of weakness, of laziness, not a medical illness," comments Martiece Carson, a neuropsychiatrist at the University of Oklahoma Health Sciences Center, Oklahoma City, in a recent article in the *New York Times*.

Q: Do children suffer from depression?

A: It's said that between 3 and 6 million people under the age of 18 suffer from clinical depression. Some researchers believe that even infants can become depressed, and depression is sometimes suggested as a factor in the so-called fail-to-thrive babies for whose problems there is no clear cause.

Q: What's the actual rate of depression in children?

A: In general, there is a low rate of depression among very young children: less than 1 percent in preschool children, and 2 percent in school-age children who haven't reached puberty. The rate is the same for boys and girls.

The onset of puberty, which can itself sometimes trigger a major depressive episode, leads to an increase in the rate of depression in both sexes. After puberty, however, the rate of depression begins to rise more steeply for girls, until it mirrors the two-to-one incidence in women.

Q: How can you tell when a young child is depressed?

A: You look for behavioral changes. For example, infants withdraw, lose interest in activities around them and may stop eating. Preschoolers may throw temper tantrums, cling to their parents and regress in speech and toilet training. School-age children may become irritable, pick fights, talk back to their parents and complain of aches and pains.

Q: But don't a lot of children act that way anyway?

A: True. All children pass through developmental stages that make it more difficult to diagnose a mental disorder. Moreover, some children who appear depressed really have behavior disorders, while others who appear to have behavior disorders are actually depressed. That's why it can be hard to diagnose depression in children, particularly when they're very young.

Recognizing the differences, the psychiatric profession has defined depressive orders differently for children so that, for example, irritability may be a more frequent symptom than depression. In addition, the symptoms of chronic depression must last for only one year for a child to be diagnosed as dysthymic.

Q: What are the signs of depression in a teenager?

A: It can be even harder to detect depression in teenagers because that's a developmental stage characterized by considerable anger and withdrawal. Psychologists say that parents should be on the lookout for depression when teenagers drop their favorite activities, cut school, do drugs or, particularly, talk of death or suicide.

DEPRESSION AND OTHER ILLNESS

Q: All right, it's miserable to be depressed. But it isn't fatal, is it?

A: It can be. There's a strong association between major depressive disorder and physical illness. Studies show that depressed individuals have more physical illnesses and use health care more than people who aren't depressed.

A recent study of two groups of hospital patients—one with depression and one without—found that the average length of stay for the group with depression was 10 days longer than for the nondepressed group. The study, which appeared in the *Journal of Clinical Psychiatry,* matched people for severity in the physical illness that had led to their hospitalization.

A report published in the *Journal of the American Medical Association* in 1991 found that patients with major depressive disorder who were admitted to nursing homes had a 59 percent greater likelihood of dying in the first year after admission than those who weren't depressed. Another study found that people who were 55 and over and had major depressive disorder had a mortality rate over the next 15 months that was four times higher than that of nondepressed people in the same age-group.

Q: Why would depression lead to physical illness?

A: The cause-and-effect relationship isn't clear, and obviously the relationship varies with the physical illness that results. But there's considerable evidence that the presence of major depressive disorder can suppress the immune system.

In addition, depression can lead to unhealthy behavior, such as heavy drinking, and may exacerbate physical problems already present.

For example, numerous recent studies have found that adults with diabetes are three times more likely to be depressed than adults who don't have diabetes. While it's not clear why some people with diabetes get depressed and others don't, it is known that the people who are diabetic and who are depressed have more problems with glucose regulation, presumably because they don't adhere as faithfully to the guidelines. Since poor glucose regulation tends to lead to increased complications, such people have a higher chance of developing more physical problems.

Q: **What about people with heart conditions? Does depression affect their long-term prospects?**

A: Evidence suggests it does. A Canadian study published in the *Journal of the American Medical Association* in 1993 found that heart-attack patients who were severely depressed were about five times as likely to die within six months of leaving the hospital as patients who weren't depressed. And a German study, published in *Lancet* in 1994, found that heart-attack patients who were depressed were twice as likely to have chest pain. In both studies, the depressed patients' heart disease wasn't more severe than that of patients who weren't depressed.

Q: **I've heard that people who get depressed are more likely to develop cancer. Is that true?**

A: While depression has been pegged as a potential cancer risk factor, the actual evidence linking the two is divided.

In laboratory studies in the 1970s, rats were caused to have "learned helplessness"—a condition associated with depression (see Chapter 2). These rats were far less capable of rejecting implanted tumors. On the other hand, a recent report by a researcher at the Kaiser Permanente Medical Care Program in Oakland, California, which followed 144,000 people for up to 19 years, found no link between depression and increased cancer risk.

Q: **You mentioned depression and overdrinking earlier. Is it true that people who are depressed are more likely to become alcoholics?**

A: Again, the cause-and-effect relationship needs closer analysis. According to the Depression Guideline Panel, most studies indicate that alcoholism is rarely a consequence of depression, although there's some indication that it may be a pattern among women.

Q: **Then does alcoholism lead to depression?**

A: The panel says that most studies have found that between 10 and 30 percent of alcoholics do become depressed over time. One possible reason may be that prolonged intoxication alters the brain chemistry.

Then there's the purely anecdotal evidence offered by the writer William Styron, who went into a deep depression in 1985. In his book *Darkness Visible: A Memoir of Madness,* Styron speculates that his depressive disorder may actually have been triggered by his abrupt withdrawal from alcohol, which he'd abused for years. In his view, alcohol had acted as "a shield against anxiety." When it was suddenly withdrawn, he became vulnerable to the depression that, due to

genetic and other factors in his personal history, "had
hovered near me for years, waiting to swoop down."

Q: What about drug abuse? Is there a link between it and depression?

A: Actually, major depression has a significantly greater
association with drug dependency—particularly
opiate, prescription and stimulant dependency—than it does
with alcohol. A study headed by Mark S. Gold, M.D., a
psychiatrist at the University of Florida, found that the more
drugs people used and the more frequently they used them,
the likelier they were to have major depressive disorder.
Daily drug users showed the greatest incidence of depression.

Q: Are there other psychiatric conditions that people who are depressed are more likely to develop?

A: There are a number of psychiatric conditions that
frequently overlap with major depressive disorder.
According to the Depression Guideline Panel, up to 43 percent of people with major depressive disorder have histories
of one or more "nonmood" psychiatric disorders: In addition
to alcoholism, the other conditions often associated with
depression include **anxiety disorder**, **panic disorder** or
phobic disorder, eating disorders (either **bulimia** or
anorexia nervosa) and **obsessive-compulsive disorders**.
For example, the panel notes, one-third to one-half of patients
with eating disorders also have major depressive disorder at
the same time, and approximately 50 to 75 percent of patients
with eating disorders have a lifetime history of major depressive disorder.

Q: Why is there such a high correlation between depression and other mental illnesses?

A: In many cases, it would appear that another psychiatric condition may have precipitated depression. People suffering from anorexia, for example, often exhibit a number of depressive symptoms, all of which usually improve once they start eating properly and regaining weight.

In the case of an anxiety, panic or phobic disorder, it's hard to generalize about a causal relationship. Genetics seems to play some role; people with **agoraphobia**, for example, tend to have a significant family history of mood disorders.

What is clear is that, when people who are depressed also have panic disorder, it worsens and prolongs their illnesses and raises their risks for suicide.

Q: What is the risk of suicide in depression?

A: One widely cited statistic is that 15 percent of depressed individuals who aren't being treated or whose depression isn't responding to treatment commit suicide. In 1990, about 15,000 men and 3,400 women in the United States committed suicide because of depression, according to a report in the *Journal of Clinical Psychiatry.* A study from the University of California at San Diego has suggested that the rate may be even higher; many deaths caused by "accidental" drug overdoses may actually be suicides.

Another way to put it is that, by conservative estimates, at least 50 percent of suicides can be attributed to major depressive disorder; some researchers put the figure much higher.

Q: Who's at greatest risk for committing suicide?

A: According to the NIH, the suicide rate among older people—80- to 84-year-olds—was 26.5 per 100,000 persons in 1988, more than double the rate for the general population. Elderly white men are at highest risk.

According to the NIH, most of the men were suffering from their first episode of major depression, which was only moderately severe, but their symptoms had gone unrecognized and untreated. A discussion of treatment—or nontreatment, as the case may be—of the elderly appears in Chapter 3.

Q: What about children? Are they at risk for suicide?

A: Suicide is still rare in children under the age of 12. However, more than 200 children between the ages of 5 and 14 commit suicide each year, and certainly many more attempt it.

The rate of completed suicides among teenagers ages 15 to 19 has tripled in the past 30 years to 100,000 annually. Suicide has become the second leading cause of death among older teenagers.

Q: Did they all commit suicide because they were depressed?

A: No, depression isn't the only factor. Extreme anxiety may be the driving force in most cases. A Chicago-area study of 70 suicides among teenagers found that only one-quarter were seriously depressed at the time, according to David C. Clark, Ph.D., of the Center for Suicide Research and Prevention at Rush-Presbyterian-St. Luke's Medical Center, Chicago.

However, David Brent, M.D., a child psychiatrist at the University of Pittsburgh who is also an expert in this area, says depression raises a teenager's risk of completed suicide thirtyfold. "Affective disorder is the most significant and predominant risk factor in adolescent suicide," Brent concluded in a recent study.

2 CAUSES OF DEPRESSION

Q: What causes depression?

A: The precise mechanism, or mechanisms, through which depression occurs has not yet been discovered. However, there are usually a number of factors, both biochemical and **psychosocial**, that combine to bring about depression.

It's arguable that some men and women, because of their biochemical/genetic makeups, are inherently more susceptible to depression than other people who are exposed to the same environmental or social factors. It's also been suggested that, even when depression doesn't have a physiological cause, chronic depression can lead to neurological change—and that, in turn, can enhance a person's propensity for depression.

BIOLOGICAL CAUSES

Q: What are the biochemical factors?

A: Depression and mania have been associated with improper functioning of certain **neurotransmitters**

—chemical "messengers" in the brain that transmit electrical signals from one nerve cell to another across the **synapse**, or space between cells. This transmission of signals sets in motion the complex neural interactions that shape our behaviors, feelings and thoughts.

Scientists have believed for years that depression is related to a deficit of neurotransmitters—either the chemicals **norepinephrine** or **serotonin**—at critical synapses in the central nervous system. In experiments with animals and humans, an increase in serotonin has been associated with less aggression, irritability and impulsive behavior.

On the other hand, it's believed that mania, the flip side of depression, is related to an excess of those neurotransmitters.

Q: So it's only two neurotransmitters that may be involved?

A: Researchers are now finding that at least one more neurotransmitter chemical, **dopamine**, may also be involved in mood disorders. And since there are some 100 other neurotransmitters with functions that have yet to be determined, it's possible the key biochemical cause of depression is still unknown.

Q: Are there biochemical factors besides neurotransmitters?

A: Other studies have examined the possibility that people with depressive disorder may have neuro-endocrine abnormalities. The endocrine system is the body's network of glands—for example, the thyroid gland, located in the neck. These glands release hormones into the bloodstream.

People with endocrine disorders often appear to have mood disorders; hyperthyroidism (increased thyroid function) can cause symptoms similar to mania, while hypothyroidism (reduced thyroid function) may suggest depression. In both cases, however, symptoms can be eliminated by correcting the hormonal imbalance.

Q: Then endocrine disorders don't actually cause depression, just depressive symptoms?

A: One endocrine system, the hypothalamic-pituitary-adrenal (HPA) axis, is under investigation as a possible cause of depression. (The hypothalamus is that part of the brain that regulates hormone balance as well as sleep cycles, appetite, thirst and complex emotional behaviors.)

The HPA axis is involved in the regulation of **cortisol**, a steroid hormone that is secreted during prolonged stress of any kind. In studies involving patients with either unipolar or bipolar depression, researchers have found that about half had elevated levels of cortisol in their blood or urine. Those levels returned to normal when the patients recovered from their depressions.

Q: Can doctors reduce levels of cortisol with medication?

A: Normally, the administration of **dexamethasone**, a synthetic steroid, suppresses the production of cortisol. But in about half of depressed patients, that doesn't do the trick. It wasn't until an individual recovered from depression that his cortisol level and dexamethasone suppression test (DST) returned to normal.

Q: If a high cortisol level is related to depression, that sounds like a good way to diagnose depression. Is it?

A: No, it's too inexact. For one thing, the DST fails to identify many people who are depressed. For another, many people with abnormally high levels of cortisol have disorders other than depression.

Q: You mentioned that genetics can play a part. Is depression inherited?

A: Studies of families with an unusually high incidence of depressive illness have led scientists to conclude that there's a genetic predisposition to some forms of depression, particularly those that recur.

It's been found that if one identical twin suffers from depression or mania, there is a 70 to 80 percent likelihood that the other twin will, too. Nonidentical twins, just like siblings, parents or children of a person with depression, run a risk of about 25 percent. Since identical twins have all their genes in common, the higher rate indicates a strong genetic factor.

According to the American Psychiatric Association, major depression occurs 1½ to 3 times as often among those with a first-degree biological relative (a parent, grandparent or sibling) affected with the disorder as among the general population.

Q: But couldn't environment account for that?

A: The genetic factor appears to be the determining factor, judging from studies of people who were adopted. Two of those studies, by researchers in New York and Brussels, identified two groups of adopted individuals:

those who had been diagnosed as having a depressive illness and those who had not.

Researchers found that the biological relatives of adoptees with depressive illnesses had higher rates of major depressive illnesses, alcoholism and suicide than did relatives of adoptees who weren't depressed. The Belgian study also reported that there was a greater degree of affective illness in the biological parents of these adoptees than in their adoptive parents.

A study in Denmark, which included first- and second-degree relatives of both biological and adopting families of depressed individuals, found that the incidence of depression was three times greater among biological relatives than in the adopting families.

Q: Is manic depression genetic, too?

A: Actually, bipolar depression—as the medical profession prefers to call it—has a far greater genetic element than unipolar depression. First-degree relatives of people with the most common type of manic depression have a 12 percent chance of having the same disorder over their lifetimes. (That compares with approximately 1 percent for the general population.)

Another 12 percent have recurrent major depressive disorder, and yet another 12 percent have dysthymia or other mood disorders. In other words, more than one-third of the close relatives of people with manic depression themselves may have a mood disorder of one type or another during their lives.

Q: Do scientists know which genes are responsible?

A: No, although they're actively investigating the precise genetic mechanisms, particularly for bipolar disorder. One complication is that most scientists believe

manic depression involves several genes, although how many genes and what they do, researchers can't say.

Recently scientists at Johns Hopkins Hospital, Baltimore, Maryland, announced a stunning discovery: In some of the families they'd followed, every woman with manic depression passed it on to her children, but not one man with the disorder passed it along. The researchers hypothesized that manic depression is linked to mitochondrial DNA, a fragment outside the cell's nucleus. Only a mother's mitochondrial genes are passed on to a child.

However, the hypothesis doesn't fit all the families Hopkins has been studying. And it's worth remembering the Amish study we mentioned in Chapter 1. After researchers announced they'd located the manic-depressive gene, two previously healthy subjects developed mood disorders—and the findings fell apart.

Q: So then, what can we conclude about the genetic link in depression?

A: We can conclude that it's significant but, as a recent study published in the *American Journal of Psychiatry* proved yet again, genetics is only one factor. Kenneth Kendler, M.D., a professor of psychiatry and human genetics at the Medical College of Virginia Commonwealth University, examined 680 pairs of female twins in the context of several basic variables thought to be risk factors for depression: recent life stressors, genetics, previous history of depression, inner emotional conflict, parental warmth, lifetime traumas (for example, rape or sexual abuse), social support and parental loss.

Kendler found that the first four factors were the strongest predictors of whether someone would develop depression. And of all the factors, recent stress—divorce, illness or bereavement, for example—was the best predictor of a depressive episode. Genetic factors, he concluded, play a "substantial but not overwhelming role" in causing major depression.

Q: What about other biological causes? Aren't there diseases that lead to depression?

A: Many medical disorders produce some of the symptoms of depression, including weight loss, sleep disturbances and low energy. In addition to certain types of cancer, these disorders include diabetes, hypothyroidism, kidney or liver dysfunction; some infections, such as AIDS; some neurologic conditions, such as stroke and Parkinson's disease; cardiovascular disease; and deficiency of certain minerals or vitamins, particularly vitamins B_6, B_{12} and folate.

The prevalence of these problems among the elderly is one reason older people may appear depressed. However, if they're being treated for these ailments, the treatment should also eliminate the depression.

Still other illnesses, many of which afflict younger people, produce the same symptoms as depression: mononucleosis, Epstein-Barr disease, chronic fatigue syndrome. And a manic or depressed state has been known to follow head injury, with manic states usually resulting from injury to the right hemisphere of the brain.

Q: It seems natural to be depressed if you're seriously ill. Is that actually a disorder?

A: It's common for serious illness to lead to depression, particularly if there's chronic pain, but it's still a mood disorder. Terminal cancer patients also experience high rates of depression, and major depression occurs in 25 percent of cancer patients in general.

A recent study at Memorial Sloan-Kettering Cancer Center in New York found that ineffective treatment of pain is a major reason cancer patients become depressed or suicidal. "They became suicidal not because of how much pain they were having, but because the doctor was not doing very well in terms of relieving their pain," says William Breitbart, who directed the study.

Q: What about heart disease? Is that associated with depression?

A: Yes, it's common for people who've had heart attacks and open-heart surgery to experience depression. The German study in *Lancet* of 377 male heart-attack patients, for example, found that 13 percent were severely depressed and 23 percent moderately depressed six months after their attacks. That's greater by about a factor of 10 than the incidence of depression among men overall.

The connection is partly psychological rather than biological. For one thing, they face terrible odds; according to the Framingham Group Study—the biggest, longest-running heart study in America—of those people who survive a coronary, one-third die within two years. For another, it's said that survivors of open-heart surgery may be particularly depressed by the fact their heart—the real and metaphorical center of their being—has been invaded.

Q: What other diseases are associated with depression?

A: People who've had strokes often become depressed. The precise reason isn't clear; studies have found only a weak relationship between the depression's severity and the level of physical and cognitive impairment. In some patients, depression may be related to the injury, particularly if the stroke involved the front of the left hemisphere of the brain.

Whatever the cause, stroke patients who become depressed don't recover as well from their strokes as those who aren't depressed: Case reports indicate they comply less with treatment, and are more irritable and demanding.

Q: Are there drugs—legal drugs—that cause depression?

A: A number of medications have been reported to induce depression in some cases. These include cardiovascular drugs, such as digitalis; psychotropics, such as benzodiazepine; some agents to treat infection, inflammation or cancer; and hormonal treatments, such as oral contraceptives (because of their progesterone content) and anabolic steroids. One researcher has described two cases of women with no psychiatric history who developed major depression within one or two months after insertion of Norplant, the long-acting contraceptive that is implanted under the skin.

Withdrawal from drugs that are stimulants, such as cocaine and amphetamines, can also lead to symptoms of depression, such as sadness, insomnia and apathy.

PSYCHOSOCIAL CAUSES

Q: Are there depressions that don't have a physical basis?

A: The biochemical proponents tend to argue that all serious depression has a physical cause. The other extreme—the Freudian view that for years dominated the medical community's view of depression—was that depression was purely psychological in nature. The truth is probably somewhere in the middle.

Q: What's the Freudian view?

A: Sigmund Freud, the founder of **psychoanalysis**, theorized that depression was the unexpressed and

unconscious rage that developed as a reaction to being helpless or dependent on others or to the loss of a loved one.
A child's earliest rage might be caused by his feeling of
"abandonment" by his mother when she has another child.
Because he cannot afford to rage against his mother and risk
antagonizing her, Freud theorized, the child turns the anger
against himself. Thus the unexpressed anger is bottled up,
or internalized.

In short, anger turned inward produces depression. And
each subsequent time the individual is again faced with
abandonment, he becomes depressed.

Q: Does anyone still believe this?

A: The theory has fallen out of favor at the moment, as
has psychoanalysis, a psychotherapeutic method that
is more an art than a science and whose efficacy has never
been established. But while many of Freud's theories have
lost standing in the psychiatric community, others are still
widely accepted.

For example, Freud theorized back in 1917 that a child
who lost her mother at an early age through death or separation would be susceptible to depression as an adult. Recently,
George W. Brown, a sociologist at the University of London
who conducted research in working-class London neighbor-
hoods in the 1960s, backed up Freud by asserting that the
death of one's mother before a girl reaches her teens makes
her particularly prone to depression.

However, Brown offered a social as well as a psychological
explanation. He suggested that the mother's death not only
could erode the girl's feelings of control and self-esteem, it
might increase the girl's chance of "untoward experiences,"
such as unhappy relationships and bad marriages.

Q: Just girls? What about boys who lose their mothers?

A: Brown was studying the incidence of depression in women. However, there are indications—based on anecdotal evidence rather than studies—that men are also affected by such loss.

For example, in his memoir, *Darkness Visible,* writer William Styron cites the death of his mother when he was only 13—and his failure to mourn her fully at the time—as a contributing factor in his major depression. And a social historian, Howard I. Kushner, in *Self-Destruction in the Promised Land,* has suggested that Abraham Lincoln's frequent bouts of melancholy were linked to the death of his mother when he was nine.

Q: What other psychosocial factors are involved in depression?

A: As we indicated earlier, studies suggest that stress is a trigger for depression. Stressors that contribute to depression are defined as major life events, such as a death in the family, not the day-to-day minutiae, like rush-hour traffic, to which everybody is subject all the time. (While psychologically disturbed people may react violently to those stresses —witness the occasional shootings on freeways or in gas-station lines—otherwise healthy individuals generally take them in stride.)

Q: Is there a way to predict risk for depression from stress?

A: You can measure the stress in your life with the Stress Scale, developed by University of Washington medical school researchers Thomas H. Holmes and Richard H. Rahe in 1965. While the scale was designed to rate an individual's risk for illness in general, it is widely regarded as a useful predictor of depression.

Here are the "events" on the scale, with their "value":

Death of spouse	100
Divorce	73
Marital separation	65
Jail term	63
Death of close family member	63
Personal injury or illness	53
Marriage	50
Fired from work	47
Marital reconciliation	45
Retirement	45
Change in family member's health	44
Pregnancy	40
Sex difficulties	39
Addition to family	39
Business readjustment	39
Change in financial status	38
Death of close friend	37
Change to different line of work	36
Change in number of marital arguments	36
Mortgage or loan over $10,000	31
Foreclosure of mortgage or loan	30
Change in work responsibilities	29
Son or daughter leaving home	29
Trouble with in-laws	29
Outstanding personal achievement	28
Spouse begins or stops work	26
Starting or finishing school	26
Change in living conditions	25

Revision of personal habits	24
Trouble with boss	23
Change in work hours, conditions	20
Change in residence	20
Change in schools	20
Change in recreational habits	19
Change in church activities	19
Change in social activities	18
Mortgage or loan under $10,000	17

"The Social Readjustment Rating Scale" reprinted with permission from *Journal of Psychomatic Research,* Volume 11, T.H. Holmes and R.H. Rahe, 1967, Elsevier Science Ltd., Pergamon Imprint, Oxford, England.

Q: **But aren't some of these stresses pretty nice?**

A: As you can see, even "positive" or pleasant stressors can be factors in depression. Not only do marriage and marital reconciliation make the list, there are such seemingly unambiguously good experiences as "outstanding personal achievement."

Nor are they all earth-shattering. There are also relatively minor events, such as taking out a small mortgage or loan.

Q: **How do I measure my stress level?**

A: From the list, you check those "events" that you've experienced during the previous 12 months. If you score above 300, you are deemed to be at high risk for depression and other illnesses.

Q: But surely it's natural to be sad if you lose a husband or wife?

A: Yes, but it's unhealthy if that grieving turns into a major depression. A study of recent widows and widowers by Sidney Zisook, professor of psychiatry at the University of California, San Diego, School of Medicine, found that one-fourth met established psychiatric criteria for major depression two months after the loss of a spouse; two years later, 14 percent remained deeply depressed.

At the two-month mark, the American Psychiatric Association says, the condition should no longer be characterized as an "uncomplicated bereavement," the APA's term for normal grieving. When depression occurs, "even in the context of severe life stress," says Zissok, it should be treated.

Q: So all major stresses can lead to depression?

A: There's stress, and there's stress. While significant events can be stressful, the day-to-day stresses to which many people who lead otherwise fulfilling lives are subject are actually good for them, evidence suggests. Psychologists have an "enhancement" hypothesis that argues that occupying multiple roles—for example, being a wife, mother *and* career woman—can actually enhance one's feelings of security and self-worth. (For more, see the section on women in this chapter.)

Q: Do certain stresses lead to different types of depression?

A: A University of Tennessee study found that people with chronic depression were significantly more likely to have a disabled spouse, multiple losses of immediate family members through death, and concurrent disabling medical conditions, such as rheumatic or cardiovascular diseases.

Q: Is there always something that triggers depression?

A: Not always. Sometimes depression comes on suddenly and without any apparent cause. However, a study by psychiatrist Alan Romanoski, M.D., at Johns Hopkins University, using data gathered from 800 local residents, found that 86 percent of major depressions were precipitated by a real-life event or situation; the others were without apparent cause.

Q: What psychosocial factors besides stress cause depression?

A: Psychologists say that a lack of social support or friends may exacerbate a tendency toward depression —or, put another way, a strong network of friends can help protect one from depression.

That appears to be particularly true of certain age-groups, such as college students who are in a transitional stage between their own families and their future families. A recent study of depression among college students by researchers at the University of Toronto found that the presence of social support, almost always in the form of a confidant, was the most important factor in determining whether a student became depressed or not.

But the need for friends isn't limited to the young. Research has also shown that for older adults, social support becomes most important when they experience a high level of stress. The need for social support is a significant risk factor for the elderly, who are continually losing close relatives or friends to illness or death—itself a stressful experience.

Q: You said earlier that some people are more susceptible to depression than others. Are certain personality types more prone to depression?

A: Some researchers believe there's a syndrome called "depressive personality disorder." People with this disorder tend to be pessimistic and brooding, critical of themselves and others. They see the world as cruel and unsupportive, themselves as unworthy and the future as hopeless. Because of their essentially negative view of life, they're predisposed to depression.

Q: What makes people that way?

A: It's believed that particularly painful experiences early in life may give individuals a predisposition to depression. One theory is that such experiences literally etch themselves in the brain, altering an individual's neurochemistry and placing him at higher risk for depression.

These experiences may include the loss of a parent or simply the tumult of divorce. An adoption study by researchers in Copenhagen suggests that being raised by an alcoholic parent can increase one's vulnerability to depression; still other studies have focused on girls with alcoholic fathers. Other early experiences that can set the stage for a lifetime of depression obviously include abuse, physical and/or sexual.

Q: Does that mean that people who develop major depressions truly had harder childhoods?

A: That's a somewhat controversial issue among psychologists, at least when it comes to generalizations rather than specific individuals and traumatic events.

One school of thought is that people who are depressed cannot provide an accurate picture of their lives precisely because they're depressed. Peter Lewinsohn, Ph.D., a psychologist with the Oregon Research Institute, Eugene, says that while depressed people recall that their parents were rejecting, those harsh recollections tend to dissipate when the depression lifts. On the other hand, in his book *Learned Optimism,* Martin Seligman, director of clinical training in psychology at the University of Pennsylvania, Philadelphia, describes laboratory experiments in which he tested the recall of depressed and nondepressed people. He concludes that depressed people tend to remember things accurately, while nondepressed people distort the past by casting it in a more favorable light!

Q: **Then if it's not an unhappy youth, what would make someone predisposed to depression?**

A: It's possible that a person simply learned a pattern of pessimistic, negative thinking as she was growing up. There's a psychological theory called "learned helplessness" that has been widely adopted as an explanation of why some people become depressed.

Q: **What is "learned helplessness"?**

A: The theory was developed in the 1960s by Seligman who, as a young graduate assistant in experimental psychology, noted that dogs who were exposed to mild shocks over which they had no control—the shocks went on and off regardless of whether or not they jumped or barked—eventually gave up trying to get away from the shocks. They simply lay down and whimpered.

Subsequent experiments by Seligman and other investigators established that the same response of learned helplessness could be produced in humans. One group of people was allowed to bring some event—noise, shock, light—under control while another group had no effect. "The helpless group gave up," said Seligman. "They became so passive that even in new situations, they didn't try."

Q: What does that have to do with depression?

A: Seligman and his colleagues then tested the subjects, animal and human, against the American Psychiatric Association's nine criteria for diagnosing depression. They found that most of the helpless subjects showed every symptom except the ninth, a suicidal tendency—and that, Seligman suggested, "was probably only because the laboratory failures were so minor," like failing to turn off noise or solve anagrams. Depression, he concluded, "could be caused by defeat, failure and loss and the consequent belief that any actions taken will be futile."

Q: Okay, but let's take this out of the laboratory. What does it mean in real life?

A: In real life, people become prey to helplessness by the way they explain things to themselves—what psychologists call their "explanatory style" or "attribution style." When depressed people do well at something, they attribute it to luck; when they fail, they take all the blame.

According to Seligman, there are three crucial dimensions to explanatory style:

• Permanence. Pessimists believe bad events are permanent ("I'm all washed up"); optimists think they're transitory ("I'm exhausted").

• Pervasiveness. Pessimists make universal explanations for their failures ("All teachers are unfair"); optimists make specific explanations ("That teacher is unfair").

• Personalization. When bad things happen, pessimists blame themselves ("I'm stupid"); optimists blame others or external events ("You're stupid").

Q: **What's the evidence that a negative explanatory style leads to depression?**

A: More than 200 published studies have examined the role of a negative or pessimistic explanatory style in depression, and generally support the relationship. One study specifically asked whether a pessimistic explanatory style preceded depression or merely accompanied it, and concluded that people are more apt to develop depression if they start with a more pessimistic style.

Q: **Is there any evidence of a physiological link between learned helplessness and depression?**

A: In a recent study at the University of Tuebingen in Germany, experimenters induced learned helplessness in 12 otherwise healthy individuals by giving them unsolvable cognitive problems. Through a series of brain scans, they found that the experiment caused a change in specific regions of the brain. While the researchers couldn't connect that result to depression, the finding suggests that learned helplessness may have potentially long-lasting functional implications.

DEPRESSION IN WOMEN

Q: Why is the rate of depression so much higher in women?

A: As we indicated in Chapter 1, there's some debate over whether it is actually higher in women.
However, according to the American Psychological Association's 1990 Task Force Report on Women and Depression, women "truly are more depressed than men, primarily due to their experience of being female in our contemporary culture." The report went on to cite a variety of biological, social and psychological factors unique to women that cut across racial and class lines.

Q: Let's start with the biological factors. What are they?

A: A number of reproduction-related events—infertility, miscarriage, childbirth—as well as the use of birth-control pills, have been linked to depression in women. Precise cause-and-effect isn't fully understood; there's mixed evidence regarding the influence of fluctuations in female hormones and other biochemicals on mood, and reproductive events have a strong psychological as well as biological component. But whatever the cause, it's clear that these events trigger major depressive episodes in many women.

Q: Is that what postpartum blues are?

A: "The blues," which are said to occur in 50 to 80 percent of all new mothers, is a brief period of weepiness or letdown after the emotionally charged experience of birth.

But in about 10 percent of new mothers, a more severe and longer-lasting depression known as **postpartum depression (PPD)** sets in, between one week and six months after the birth.

Q: How serious is postpartum depression?

A: Like any major depression, it can be debilitating enough to require hospitalization. The condition can interfere with the mother's ability to bond with her newborn and hamper her ability to look after the new baby. There is some evidence that infants of such mothers may suffer long-term emotional and mental development.

In addition, one or two new mothers in 1,000 may suddenly develop a serious form of PPD called postpartum psychosis, which requires immediate medical help. Symptoms include hallucinations, delusions, suicidal thoughts and attempts to harm the baby. Tragically, there have been rare cases where women with postpartum psychosis have killed their newborns.

Q: What causes postpartum depression?

A: There have been attempts to find psychological underpinnings, but researchers have found only a slim connection at best between PPD and an ambivalent or anxious attitude regarding pregnancy or motherhood. It is now known that women who are depressed while pregnant have a greater risk of developing a mood disorder after childbirth.

Most scientists assume there's a hormonal component; indeed, studies have found that women with postpartum depression have significantly higher levels of cortisol. However, they've yet to find a specific biological mechanism that would explain hormonal involvement.

Q: Isn't PMS (premenstrual syndrome) associated with depression?

A: Menstrual cycles and PMS specifically have been associated with depressed feelings and irritability, but psychiatrists exclude PMS as a source of major depressive disorder. Women who are depressed, however, usually find that their symptoms worsen in the premenstrual period, according to *How to Cope With Depression,* co-authored by J. Raymond DePaulo Jr., M.D., a psychiatrist at Johns Hopkins Center for Affective Disorders.

Q: But doesn't the menstrual cycle ever trigger depression?

A: Yes, in some 3 to 5 percent of menstruating women there's a cyclic mood disorder known as **premenstrual dysphoric disorder (PMDD)**. PMDD involves a pattern of severe, recurrent symptoms of depression and other negative mood states. It typically occurs in the last week of the menstrual cycle and can disappear once menstruation begins. The condition is far more disabling than PMS.

Q: Does menopause lead to depression?

A: Not as a rule, although it may often appear that way. Many menopausal symptoms—difficulty sleeping, fatigue, irritability—parallel depressive symptoms. Furthermore, research has found that depressed women are twice as likely to report menopausal symptoms, such as hot flashes, and are more likely to seek medical help for menopausal symptoms than are nondepressed women. As a result, it was once thought that menopause and the "empty-nest" syndrome induced depression.

More recent research suggests that isn't the case, however, and that many women find menopause liberating. But not all. One study reported that women who became the most distressed at menopause were those who'd relied on their childbearing and child-rearing roles for status and self-esteem.

Q: **You've discussed social and psychological factors that often lead to depression. Are there factors that are unique to women?**

A: "Stress is ubiquitous in women's lives—from poverty and violence, to name just two sources," the American Psychological Association Task Force reported. Poverty has been described as a "pathway to depression"—money problems and job loss are frequently cited as risk factors—and 75 percent of people living below the poverty line in the United States are women and children.

In addition, women suffer to a disproportionate share of the violence in our society, from childhood sexual abuse to rape and wife battering. Some of this violence may cause neurological changes that result in depressive symptoms, but in most cases depression is attributed to the psychology of what the Task Force calls "victimization."

Researchers have found that women who were the victims of incest and rape as children tend to exhibit helplessness, rage and self-blame—characteristics also associated with depression. A 1991 Stanford University study suggests that one-third of the difference between the rates of depression for men and women is due to the sexual abuse of women as children. Other studies have found extremely high rates of depression in women who have been raped or battered.

Q: Can childhood sexual abuse really depress someone years later—particularly if there's no memory of it happening?

A: You've touched on an extremely controversial area of psychotherapy. Recently there have been a number of cases of women who suffered from depression for many years suddenly "recovering" the repressed memory of a traumatic event in their childhoods. In most cases, they've recalled the event—usually incest—with the help of a psychotherapist.

Some mental-health professionals believe that many of these women have been misled by their therapists into recovering memories that are actually false. In other cases, the accuracy of these memories has even been upheld in court. Whatever the overall merits of recovered memory, it's generally agreed that some women may be depressed by past traumas of which they have no conscious memory.

Q: Okay, but most women aren't victims of violence. What other factors account for the high rate of depression?

A: Researchers cite such stress factors as bad marriages or relationships, the absence of the husband, social isolation and being homebound with young children.

Q: Aren't people who are married less prone to depression?

A: That depends on whether or not it's a good marriage. Studies have shown that husbands are generally more satisfied with their marriages than wives are, and that women who are unhappily married experience more depressive symptoms than either happily married or unmarried women.

In unhappy marriages, according to these studies, women were three times more likely than men to be depressed, and almost half of all women in unhappy marriages were depressed. In happy marriages, the incidence of depression was much lower, but even so, women were almost five times more likely than men in such marriages to experience depression.

Q: And children make it worse?

A: That depends on the circumstances, of course, but studies have shown that stay-at-home mothers of young children are very vulnerable to depression, and the more children a woman has, the more likely it is she'll be depressed.

By the same token, people who stay at home to look after aging parents tend to suffer a high incidence of depression, and most of those people are women. Several studies have found depression rates of 50 percent or more among care givers of the "frail" elderly—that is, elderly people whose memories and physical capabilities are impaired by Alzheimer's disease, Parkinson's, stroke or other illnesses.

Q: So working outside the home overcomes depression?

A: The relation between women's work outside of the home and the incidence of depression is a bit more complex than that. Several studies have shown that women—young army wives in one case, middle-aged and predominantly middle-class women in another—who had been unemployed, received an appreciable psychological boost when they got a paying job.

Q: What happens when the novelty wears off?

A: That depends on a number of variables that mostly add up to one factor: the total amount of stress in the women's lives.

One critical factor seems to be supportive husbands. Researchers found that when husbands helped with child care, women benefitted from employment. In contrast, working mothers with sole responsibility for child care and difficulties arranging it had extremely high depression levels.

Similarly, Carol Aneshensel, a professor of public health at the University of California at Los Angeles who examined the effects on women of strain from marriage and jobs, found that the least depressed women were employed wives with low marital strain and low employment strain. The most depressed were nonemployed wives with high marital strain, but right above them were women who had high strain in both marriage and job.

Q: But a lot of men have the same family strains. Why should women be so adversely affected?

A: In general, men seem less affected by these issues. One study, for example, reports that having children and access to child care had no effect on husbands.

As for the impact of marriage, psychologists say that women are more affected because interpersonal roles and relationships are far more important to them than to men. Research has also found that, while women get substantial satisfaction from friendships and other relationships, they're more affected when bad things happen to other people— not only to their immediate families, but to members of their social network. As the Task Force put it, "Women's greater 'range of caring' exposes them to a greater risk of depression."

Q: What other aspects of women's psychology makes them more prone to depression?

A: Passivity, dependence and low self-esteem—traits generally ascribed to what psychologists call a "feminine personality"—are often associated with depression. Another typically feminine characteristic, they say, is a tendency to dwell, or ruminate, on feelings. Susan Nolen-Hoeksema, Ph.D., an associate professor of psychology at Stanford University, has theorized that the gender gap in depression may be due partly to the fact that women ruminate about the causes of their moods while men take actions that distract them from their moods.

Q: What about learned helplessness? Is that a factor?

A: While there are no hard data to that effect, there's plenty of evidence that girls are taught helplessness at an early age while boys are taught mastery and self-reliance.

Several studies of child-rearing practices in the 1970s found that the actions of boys more frequently had consequences than the actions of girls. While the boys were punished for aggression, they were also rewarded for good behavior. In contrast, an observational study of nursery schools found that for little girls even temper tantrums were ignored.

"This is the ultimate in helplessness, and is reminiscent of clinical descriptions of the impotent rage of the angry depressive," writes Lenore Sawyer Radloff, former research psychologist at NIMH's Center for Epidemiological Studies.

Q: Do women who are successful professionally get depressed, too?

A: While there's not much research in that area, studies indicate that professional women—chemists, nurses,

physicians, medical students, pharmacists and psychologists—
have a higher risk for suicide than women generally, and a
leading cause of suicide is depression.

Q: Why do professional women get depressed?

A: Psychologists suggest that professional women have
to grapple with several difficult issues, notably sex
discrimination and conflicts between their professional roles
and their roles as wives and mothers.

Perhaps more fundamentally, many women have trouble
with their own success. Research has shown that women are
more likely than men to attribute their success to luck or
other factors, rather than claiming credit for their achieve-
ments. "Females were less likely than males to expect to
succeed in the future, and were less likely to attempt to
succeed," notes Radloff, who compares this to the attribution style of depressed people.

Q: With all that, why aren't even more women
depressed?

A: In a sense, they may be. Alan Romanoski of Johns
Hopkins says that women suffer from moderate
depressions at 10 times the rate men do.

While that sounds alarming, some psychologists suggest
that women's propensity to mild depression—or their willing-
ness to admit to feelings of sadness—may actually prevent
the development of more severe clinical depression.

In her book *When Feeling Bad Is Good,* Ellen McGrath, a
psychologist who chaired the American Psychological Association's Task Force on Women and Depression, describes
this phenomenon as "healthy depression." She defines it as
"realistic feelings of pain, sadness and disappointment

(accompanied at times by guilt, anger and/or anxiety) from negative experiences such as traumas, losses, discrimination, unfair treatment and unresolved past damage." While "unhealthy depression" is disabling and severe, McGrath says, healthy depression can be resolved through awareness and action, and converted into energy, creativity and power.

THE ELDERLY AND CHILDREN

Q: Why do old people get depressed?

A: As we indicated earlier in this chapter, many of the causes are physical. A number of age-related illnesses and medications that the elderly take, such as drugs to lower blood pressure or relieve arthritis, may trigger depression or cause mood changes.

Research has shown, for example, that about one-fourth to one-third of people with Alzheimer's disease become clinically depressed at some point in the course of their illness—especially early on, when they're more aware of the disease's inexorable progress. Such reactions are distinct from symptoms of Alzheimer's, like forgetfulness or difficulty concentrating, that mimic depression.

Q: What about psychosocial factors?

A: Many of the major stressors that lead to depression occur most often to the elderly: chronic ill health and physical disability, financial hardship, a change in lifestyle and a loss of purpose. Sometimes men who have worked hard all their lives have difficulty adjusting to retirement and may become depressed for a time. The deaths of friends and loved ones can also be a major trigger, simultaneously creating bereavement and depriving older people of the social network that supports them.

Q: In Chapter 1 you said that the rate of depression is very high among the elderly in institutions like nursing homes. Why?

A: Apart from the fact that many of the factors mentioned above—Alzheimer's, physical disability and loss—are undoubtedly concentrated in the nursing-home population, there's the strong possibility that learned helplessness may be a contributing cause.

An experiment in the 1970s by health researchers at Yale, in which they offered residents of a local nursing home more control over their daily lives, offers some interesting evidence in that regard. First-floor residents were allowed to choose movies, meals and the kinds of plants they had in their rooms; second-floor residents were given the same amenities, but the choices were made for them. Eighteen months later, the researchers reported, the group with more choice and control was more active and happier, and relatively fewer had died.

Q: I can see how elderly people would get depressed. But why should kids get depressed?

A: For many of the same reasons that adults do: genetics, biochemistry, and physical and psychosocial factors. In 1990, *Science News* described research that found that three-month-old infants of depressed mothers "developed their own brand of 'depressed' behavior, characterized by lack of smiling and a tendency to turn the head away from the mother and other adults. These babies become more

upset when they look at their mother's unresponsive face
than when they see her leave the room.''

Q: What particular stresses would trigger depression in children?

A: For children and adolescents, major stressors can
include the death of a parent or sibling, an abusive
parent, a move to a new town or neighborhood, breakup
with a boyfriend or girlfriend, or a chronic illness, although
some studies suggest that children are less likely than adults
to be depressed about their illnesses.

Divorce is a common source of depression for children.
"They conclude that, had they been more lovable, worthy or
different, the parent would have stayed," Judith Wallerstein,
Ph.D., and Sandra Blakeslee write in *Second Chances: Men,
Women, and Children a Decade After Divorce.* "In this way,
the loss of the parent and lowered self-esteem become
intertwined."

Learning disabilities, such as attention deficit disorder,
which often cause children to perform badly at school and
thus feel like failures, may also lead to depression.

Q: Why does the rate of depression rise in girls after puberty?

A: Psychologists suggest that girls may become particularly vulnerable to depression at that time because
of the high incidence of sexual abuse. In a random sample of
nearly 1,000 adult women, 12 percent said they'd been
seriously sexually abused before the age of 17 by someone
within their family, and 26 percent said they'd been abused
by someone outside the family, before the age of 17.

Whether or not those rates are valid generally—and other
studies show both much higher and lower incidence—teenage

girls may also become more vulnerable to depression for a variety of reasons related to the status of women in our society. For example, studies have found that, while boys tend to be pleased with the physical changes puberty brings, girls are more likely to be disturbed by their new shapes.

Q: So children don't require a major stress or trauma to become depressed?

A: No. There's considerable disagreement among mental-health professionals whether children who are inherently shy or withdrawn are predisposed to depression. However, all but the most resilient children may become depressed if they are "taught" to be—if they have parents who are clinically depressed, if they're emotionally neglected or abused, if they're raised in an environment in which they don't get enough positive feedback or nurturing from adults.

Interestingly, a recent study of children who were hospitalized for major depressive disorder and/or a suicide attempt concluded that their depressive symptoms improved as a result of being removed from their home environments.

SEASONAL AFFECTIVE DISORDER (SAD)

Q: What causes seasonal affective disorder?

A: The reduced sunlight in late autumn evidently triggers a change in the chemistry of the brain, and that leads to depression. Although no one understands precisely what happens, researchers believe that winter light somehow signals the brain to reduce the concentration of serotonin in the hypothalamus. Some people appear to be more sensitive than others to this change.

The serotonin theory gets some support from the tendency of people with SAD to eat a lot of carbohydrates. Because it's thought that carbohydrates cause a rise in serotonin, the speculation is that SAD patients are unconsciously medicating themselves. In Chapter 3, we discuss treatment of SAD.

It's also been suggested that SAD is caused by higher-than-average secretions of melatonin, a neurotransmitter that is normally present at night, but research findings so far are mixed.

Finally, because SAD peaks in women between puberty and menopause, it's believed that hormones may play a part in its incidence.

Q: **Is SAD hereditary, like more typical depressive disorders?**

A: There's evidence that a propensity for SAD runs in families with related psychological problems. Norman Rosenthal, M.D., an expert on SAD at NIMH, says that a family history of mood disorders, alcohol abuse and SAD itself is common in close relatives of people with SAD. An Australian study of twins suggests SAD is inherited to some degree.

Q: **Can SAD be prevented?**

A: No, but there are many ways of ameliorating the symptoms or preventing a recurrence of SAD and other forms of depression. We discuss all these in the next four chapters, which focus on the treatment of depression.

3 TREATING DEPRESSION: AN OVERVIEW

Q: Can depression be treated successfully?

A: At least 85 percent of all people with depression can be helped to a significant degree, according to the American Psychiatric Association. (We're talking here about major depressive disorder, not dysthymia, a comparatively mild but chronic depression that's notoriously resistant to treatment.)

Furthermore, early diagnosis and treatment can often dramatically reduce the length and intensity of depression. And while no one really knows whether it's possible to prevent an initial episode of depression in an individual who is believed to be at risk, there is strong evidence that, with adequate treatment, subsequent episodes can be prevented or markedly reduced in severity.

Q: How is depression treated?

A: There are two major treatments for clinical depression: **psychotherapy** and **pharmacotherapy**, or use of **antidepressants**. Often these are combined. A third

75

category, which is less frequently used, is biological treatments, which include **electroconvulsive therapy (ECT)** and **light therapy**. We discuss in detail and evaluate all these treatments in Chapters 4, 5 and 6.

Q: You've said depression is often misdiagnosed. Is it mistreated, too?

A: It's frequently untreated or mistreated. According to the National Depressive and Manic-Depressive Association, only one-fifth of people with depressive disorder get the treatment they need. Many people see four or five physicians or psychiatrists before they find one who diagnoses and treats them effectively.

Even when depression is diagnosed, tranquilizers and sleeping pills are prescribed twice as often as the right medication, according to the National Foundation for Depressive Illness. And even when the right medication is prescribed, dosages are frequently lower than those needed to achieve a therapeutic effect.

Q: Why would depression go untreated once it's diagnosed?

A: As with other health care, cost is often a factor. People who are uninsured or underinsured are likely to find that frequent therapy or medication is beyond their means.

In addition, as we indicate in Chapter 1, people often consider depression a sign of weakness and reject the diagnosis and treatment. And severe depression can actually keep its victims from seeking help, because they may lack the energy and hope for the future that are needed to take the initiative. Some depressed individuals view their symptoms as punishment or their own fault. This can be especially true if family and friends take this view.

Q: **Can't their physicians persuade these people to accept treatment?**

A: Often the problem rests with the practitioner, not with the depressed person. That's particularly the case when the person who's depressed is elderly or terminally ill.

Traditionally, for example, there's been considerable reluctance among health-care professionals to treat depressive disorders in people with conditions such as Alzheimer's disease and terminal cancer. Many physicians who treat these people believe that depression is a reasonable response to the inexorable progress of their diseases.

However, a study published recently in the *American Journal of Psychiatry* found that Alzheimer's patients who are depressed do respond to antidepressant medications or other forms of treatment.

Q: **What about elderly people who don't have Alzheimer's? Do they get treatment?**

A: By one estimate, only about 10 percent of the depressed elderly receive treatment. This can have tragic consequences. A recent study of suicides in Ontario by people age 65 years and over found that more than 86 percent of those diagnosed as depressed had gone untreated. The 13 percent that received antidepressants were usually given a type of medication that is lethal in overdose. And few of those in the study who had medical conditions, such as cancer, heart disease or stroke, had been treated for depression.

Q: **How long does it take for treatment to work?**

A: That depends on the kind of treatment and the severity of the depression. In clinical trials, 50 to

60 percent of depressed people respond measurably to any single medication within four to six weeks, and sometimes within two to four weeks after the initial dose; full relief is often achieved within four to six months. (For the others, a different medication may be necessary.)

In contrast to medication, psychotherapy alone usually produces some improvement within 6 to 8 weeks, but may require up to 12 weeks for a full effect. According to the Depression Guideline Panel, if psychotherapy has no effect at all within 6 weeks, or hasn't achieved virtually full relief within 12 weeks, the depressed person should switch to medication.

Q: **When does someone need to be hospitalized for depression?**

A: Most people can be safely treated for depression outside a hospital setting, particularly if there are friends or family available to provide physical and emotional support. However, a short stay—typically less than a month—in either a psychiatric hospital or a psychiatric unit of a general hospital may be necessary in some cases.

Q: **Such as?**

A: In their book *The Consumer's Guide to Psychotherapy,* psychologists Jack Engler and Daniel Goleman say that hospitalization should be considered if:
- the person is threatening to kill himself or others
- the person is so apathetic that he cannot feed himself
- there's evidence of severe agitation or **psychosis**
- there is a dangerous concurrent medical condition, such as severe diabetes, that the person is no longer treating properly.

Q: How can a depressed person tell when his depression is lifting?

A: He may be the last to know. Because he's often unaware of his behavior and how it appears to others when he's depressed, health-care providers tend to depend on the reports of his family and friends. In *Understanding Depression,* Donald F. Klein, M.D., and Paul H. Wender, M.D., write that "the real question is how the patient is doing in objective, descriptive terms"—how much time is he spending at activities he usually enjoys? "This is the best way of assessing change for the better or worse," the authors write, "since depressives forget not only how good they should *feel* but what they *do* when normal."

At the same time, there are purely subjective responses. Particularly people who have been severely depressed report that, when the treatment starts to take effect, it feels as if an enveloping black cloud—or the "bell jar" described by Sylvia Plath in her novel of the same name, about her suicide attempt during a major depressive episode—has finally lifted.

Some researchers have proposed the concept of the *roll-back phenomenon,* in which as the depression lifts, many of the stages and symptoms disappear in the reverse order in which they developed. However, this isn't supported by hard data.

Q: Once the depression has ended, will the person have any symptoms?

A: Residual symptoms frequently persist even after a depressive episode has ended, but they tend to be minor. He may still have a tendency to become irritable, for example, or have trouble sleeping.

A study at Massachusetts General Hospital found that there were significant differences between people who'd recently recovered from depression and a control group without any history of depression. Researchers said the recovered depressives continued to have symptoms of depression and anxiety, and had problems with cognitive functioning, social adjustment and problem-solving.

Q: If he still has a few minor symptoms, would he stop treatment anyway?

A: Probably not, but that depends on the person, his therapist or physician and the kind of treatment he had. As a rule, after **acute treatment** has eliminated most of his symptoms, he'd receive **continuation treatment** for several months to prevent a relapse. People typically stay on medication, for example, for six months. If he doesn't have any symptoms of depression (as detailed in Chapter 1) for at least four to nine months after an episode, he's deemed to have "recovered" and may stop continuation treatment.

At that point, it's possible that he would start receiving **maintenance treatment** to prevent a new episode of depression. Maintenance treatment may involve either psychotherapy or antidepressants, or both, for one year to a lifetime, depending on the likelihood of recurrence.

Q: Who should have maintenance therapy?

A: Mainly people at risk for recurrence, as described in Chapter 1. The Depression Guideline Panel gives these conditions for maintenance medication:

• three or more episodes of major depressive disorder, or two episodes plus a clear family history of bipolar disorder

• a history of recurrence within one year after previously effective treatment with medication was discontinued

• a family history of recurrent major depressive disorder

• early onset (before the age of 20) of the first episode, or

• severe, sudden or life-threatening symptoms in both episodes in the past three years.

Q: You mentioned the possibility of taking antidepressants for a lifetime. Is it really safe to stay on these drugs indefinitely?

A: Because there have been no long-term controlled trials of antidepressants, we can't give you an unequivocal yes or no. It depends partly on the nature of the medication, partly on the risk of recurrence and, as you might expect, partly on the expertise of the person giving her professional opinion. As we discuss in detail in Chapter 5, some antidepressants have side effects or long-term effects that make long-term therapy unacceptable. In addition, some mental-health experts worry that people will become addicted or immune to these drugs.

On the other hand, there are cases of people taking antidepressants safely for 30 years. And some experts feel that indefinite drug therapy may be necessary as a preventive measure for certain individuals. In one study of recurrent depression, people who stayed on the acute-stage dose for five years fared well, while those who went off almost invariably relapsed. As a result, researchers recommended that patients whose depressive episodes occur less than 30 months apart should consider preventive maintenance for at least five years.

Q: In Chapter 2, you mentioned that some women are at risk of postpartum depression. Should they be on preventive treatment?

A: One recent study recommended that women at risk of severe postpartum depression go on antidepressants immediately after giving birth. The study, by Dr. Katherine Wisner, an assistant professor of psychiatry and reproductive medicine at Case Western Reserve University, Cleveland, tested the use of antidepressants on women who had previously suffered severe postpartum depression. Most of them had taken medication for prior episodes.

The study found that only 2 of the 17 women who went on antidepressants within 24 hours of birth and continued for at least the subsequent three high-risk months had a recurrence of PPD, compared with 5 of 8 women who declined to take medication. Wisner reasoned that, as antidepressants can take two weeks or more to take effect, women who wait until they become depressed have to cope with depression and their new babies at the same time.

While some experts second Wisner's view, others argue that—given the possible risks to breast-fed infants—it's preferable to wait until the mother shows signs of PPD.

MENTAL-HEALTH PROFESSIONALS

Q: **You've said earlier that most depressed people get better without treatment. How can a person —me, for example—decide whether to seek professional help?**

A: *The Consumer's Guide to Psychotherapy* lists three factors to consider in seeking treatment:

"1. Your level of distress: Is it intense enough that you want to do something about it?

"2. Your ability to handle your problems on your own: Are you managing or do you feel the need for more support?

"3. How much your distress is affecting your personal life, your family or your work: Are your problems getting in the way of your ability to function? Are you, your family or your work suffering significantly?"

There's a fourth consideration that's implicit in these but worth stating explicitly: Are you contemplating suicide?

Q: Who should a depressed person see for treatment?

A: Most people being treated for depression are seeing physicians who aren't mental-health experts. According to A. John Rush, M.D., a psychiatrist at the University of Texas Southwest Medical Center, Dallas, and chairman of the U.S. Department of Health and Human Services' Depression Guideline Panel, 60 percent of antidepressants are now prescribed by primary-care doctors.

Q: So if the person needs medication, she'd see a medical doctor?

A: Yes, at least on a consultative basis—as opposed to regular visits. In general, only physicians can write prescriptions. Other mental-health professionals must refer depressed patients to **psychiatrists** or primary-care M.D.'s for pharmacological consultations and antidepressant medications, while continuing to work with them in psychotherapy.

However, apart from the R$_x$, she doesn't need to see a physician to treat her depression. And, in fact, she may find that other professionals specializing in mental health are better qualified to treat her.

Q: What other professionals treat depression?

A: In addition to psychiatrists, the mental-health professionals are **psychologists, clinical social workers, family therapists** and **psychiatric nurse specialists.** In addition, there's a wide range of professionals who can also help people with depression, including members of the clergy and school guidance counselors, who are trained to detect the disorder and, at the very least, to provide referrals to experts.

Q: That's quite a list. What are the differences among the mental-health practitioners?

A: Psychiatrists are physicians (M.D.'s or D.O.'s) who have completed four years of medical school and a residency in which they specialized in treating people with psychiatric problems. They must have a general medical license to practice psychiatry and may also be board-certified —an additional, but not mandatory, professional credential.

In recent years, psychiatric training has been emphasizing the physical causes of mental illness and treatment with psychopharmaceuticals. As a result, the psychiatric community is increasingly divided between so-called biological psychiatrists, or biopsychiatrists, who believe that most mental illness has a biological cause and should be treated accordingly, and psychiatrists who practice **psychodynamic therapy** and favor a more psychological orientation.

Q: What's the background of the mental-health practitioners who aren't physicians?

A: Psychologists are educated in graduate schools of psychology rather than in medical schools, and generally have a Ph.D. (doctor of philosophy) or Psy.D. (doctor of psychology), a relatively new degree. Typically a psychologist someone would see for depression would have a subspecialty in clinical or counseling psychology and would be licensed or certified by the state.

Other nonphysician practitioners include clinical social workers, who have usually taken a two-year graduate program, including fieldwork, to obtain an M.S.W. (master's in social work). Most states now license or certify social workers as independent professionals; CSW, LICSW and ACSW are among the certifications.

Family therapists, as the name suggests, are specifically trained and licensed in marital and **family therapy**, and generally have a master's degree in marriage, family and child counseling. Increasingly, states are licensing this as a separate specialty. However, psychiatrists, psychologists and clinical social workers can also offer this type of therapy.

Alternatively, a depressed person might be treated by a psychiatric nurse specialist, a registered nurse who has specialized training in treating mental or psychiatric disorders. Psychiatric nurses may practice independently or in outpatient clinics. There is no separate state certification, although they may be certified by a state nursing association.

Q: But who's the best? And what is the pecking order, based on the severity of a person's depression?

A: Degrees and diplomas obviously provide some clues to a practitioner's intellectual ability and training, but because treatment is highly personal and subjective, it's impossible to say that any one specialty is superior to another. What we can say with relative certainty is that, of all the health-care providers, only psychiatrists are familiar with the full range of antidepressants. That's important if someone's depression is particularly severe and/or that person requires medical intervention.

Q: How does a depressed person know which type of practitioner to see?

A: That depends on a great many factors, including the severity of his depression, his preference for medication or psychotherapy and, not least, how deep his pockets are. Psychiatrists are at the top end of the price spectrum, charging upward of $100 an hour. (Fees naturally vary from one region of the country to another.) Whatever the psychiatrist's fee, a person can expect to pay about half that for a clinical social worker, and somewhere in between for a psychologist.

Q: Aren't there nonfinancial factors to consider?

A: A person should feel comfortable with every health-care professional he consults, but that's particularly important when the individual is treating him for a condition like depression. He should feel that the professional is genuinely understanding and cares about him.

Here are some other factors to consider in making a choice:

• Is the therapist or physician willing to explore a variety of treatment options? To go on antidepressants, a person doesn't need a psychiatrist. But a depressed person may not want to see a psychotherapist who is unalterably opposed to medication. And he may not want to see a psychiatrist who will consider only medication.

• Does the professional resist the idea of a person seeking a second opinion about treatment?

• Is the professional prepared to meet with the depressed person's family and friends, educate them about his condition and help them in the way they relate to him?

Even if the relationship is comfortable, if the depressed person is not feeling better within three months, he should consider trying a physician or therapist with a different therapeutic approach.

Q: Would a person see a therapist only in private practice?

A: No, many people get treated in clinic settings. These may be affiliated with hospitals, medical centers, health maintenance organizations, universities, psychotherapy training institutes, community mental-health centers or agencies in the public or private sector.

One advantage of clinics is that often their fees are lower than those of therapists in private practice, and they may provide treatment based on someone's ability to pay. Unlike many therapists in private practice, they may offer a full range of services and, if it's a mood/affective disorder clinic of a training hospital, the depressed person may get the most state-of-the art, sophisticated treatment.

The drawback of clinics is that, unless it's an emergency, she may have to wait anywhere from several days to several weeks before she can see someone. In most cases, her therapist will be assigned by the clinic, and she may be treated by somebody who is still undergoing professional training, although she will be under supervision.

Q: Does health insurance cover treatments for depression?

A: That depends on each particular policy. In general, however, it's fair to say that the coverage of psycho-therapeutic treatment of mental illness is far more restrictive than coverage of medical treatment for illness, whether it's physical or mental.

That means that, while a prescription for antidepressants may be reimbursed, in whole or part, by insurance, a person can expect to pay far more out-of-pocket for psychotherapy. She may find that her policy limits reimbursement for psychotherapy to $1,000 per person per year, for example, or that it covers one-on-one therapy but won't reimburse for group or marital and family therapy.

In some states, too, the insurer may be permitted to exclude certain mental-health-care providers, such as clinical social workers, from reimbursement.

4 PSYCHOTHERAPY

Q: How does psychotherapy help depression?

A: That depends on which type of psychotherapy being considered. According to a November 1993 issue of *Time* magazine, there are now more than 200 different kinds of "talk therapy"—as psychotherapy is often described—in the U.S. mental-health marketplace, and 10 to 15 million Americans "doing some kind of talking."

Basically, most of the talk therapies fall into two categories, which we describe in detail in this chapter. The first, described variously as psychodynamic or **insight-oriented**, tries to help patients gain an insight into the roots of their problems or an increased awareness of their unconscious motivations. The other category, known as cognitive/behavioral therapy, focuses more specifically on the here-and-now of modifying the individual's behavior and/or thought processes.

However, if someone's depression is so severe that she's having trouble working or otherwise functioning, she may not have the emotional energy or intellectual ability initially for anything more taxing than **supportive therapy**, sometimes known as psychotherapeutic management.

Q: What's supportive therapy?

A: It's a short-term therapy that emphasizes supporting, not changing, the person who's depressed. The therapist may get involved in nitty-gritty aspects such as helping a depressed person schedule absences from work, organizing her time, discouraging her from making major life changes, and enlisting the support of others in her social network. The therapist may also provide **psychoeducation** for the family to help stabilize her home environment and help her family react constructively to the illness.

Q: Does psychoeducation actually make a difference?

A: Data suggest that it does. One study of people with recurrent depression found that patients were significantly less likely to relapse and markedly more willing to comply with treatment when they were exposed to a combination of an antidepressant, psychotherapy and family psychoeducation.

Q: Who provides psychotherapy?

A: All of the mental-health-care specialists we describe in Chapter 3, as well as a number of individuals we *didn't* include. Psychotherapy itself is not a licensed profession, although the psychiatrists, psychologists and clinical social workers who practice psychotherapy are licensed within their profession.

PSYCHODYNAMIC PSYCHOTHERAPY

Q: What's involved in the psychodynamic approach?

A: Psychodynamic therapy focuses on the underlying factors that are presumed to determine behavior and adjustment. It's based on the assumption that internal psychological conflicts, possibly rooted in early childhood (for example, wanting to be both independent and cared for, or feeling angry while believing that one should always be loving), are at the root of someone's depression.

Resolution of such conflicts is thought to be essential to successful treatment. A key aspect of such treatment involves bringing the conflict into the therapeutic relationship, so that the person "transfers" to the therapist her wishes, needs, fears and so forth. This process of transference helps her see the patterns of conflict that have been shaping her life.

Q: That sounds like it would take months, if not years. Does it?

A: Psychodynamic treatment can be either brief— a matter of weeks or months—or go on for years. The most notorious of these therapies is psychoanalysis, which may involve daily sessions over the course of many years.

Q: What happens in psychoanalysis?

A: It's the most open-ended and undirected of the psychodynamic approaches. The central method, free association, calls for expressing anything that comes into your mind—thoughts, feelings, memories—no matter

how trivial or embarrassing. To strict Freudians, psychoanalysis is the only way to get rid of depression, because it
forces a depressed person to peel off the layers of defensive-
ness that have built up over time and resolve the ancient
conflicts. However, that view is distinctly in the minority
these days.

Q: You mean psychoanalysis isn't used for
depression?

A: There's no evidence that psychoanalysis is effective
against depression—or, for that matter, against any
other psychological problem. In a discussion of what procedures might be covered by health-care reform, Dr. Frederick
K. Goodwin, former director of the NIMH, told *Time* magazine, "It's clear that classical psychoanalysis, which is four to
five times a week for a four- to five-year duration, will not
be covered. It won't be covered because there is no real
evidence that it works."

Q: What happens in brief psychodynamic therapy?

A: When someone begins therapy, he and his therapist
may agree to a fixed number of sessions, say, a dozen.
As in long-term psychodynamic therapy, the focus will be on
unresolved conflicts that are still shaping his life. The therapist will limit the discussion to present problems, however,
and bring in the past only if it bears directly on those
present problems.

Q: Who should undergo psychodynamic therapy?

A: According to the American Psychiatric Association, psychodynamic therapy is most effective with people who have a capacity for insight, are psychologically minded —that is, they look at behavior in terms of motives and unconscious motivation—and have a stable environment. The approach may be most suited, the association says, to individuals with a chronic sense of emptiness, harsh self-expectations together with low self-esteem, and a history of childhood abuse, loss or separation.

Q: Are there any psychodynamic therapies used specifically for depression?

A: Interpersonal psychotherapy (IPT) is a short-term —between 12 and 16 sessions—psychodynamic therapy developed specifically to treat depression. It's based on the belief that interpersonal problems or disturbed social relationships cause people to become depressed, and that, in turn, exacerbates these unhappy relationships. The goal of IPT is to help people improve the ways they interact with others and thus get their own emotional needs met.

Q: So IPT looks only at how a depressed person relates to other people?

A: IPT focuses on four major areas of interpersonal difficulty:
• losses (for example, the end of a marriage through divorce or death) and unresolved grieving
• disputes with significant others—spouses, lovers, close relatives and so on—in his life

- changes in his roles and how he adapts to those changes (for example, the transition from being actively employed to being retired)
- social-skill "deficits" that lead to isolation.

Q: How does it work?

A: Like other psychodynamic therapies, IPT involves transference: The person's relationship with her therapist becomes a gauge for other key relationships in her life. However, the focus is on the present, and the therapist seeks to help her improve troubled relationships and develop more effective ways of relating.

Q: Can you describe a session of interpersonal therapy?

A: In the first few sessions, she and her therapist would review her past and present relationships as they relate to her depression. She'd identify problem areas.

Let's say she's having trouble with her boss—a problem she's encountered at several jobs. The therapist would ask: "Why isn't the relationship working? What do you think is the proper role of a boss? What are your functions and what are your boss's? Could you be acting this way because you unconsciously want to be fired? Do you give people a chance?"

The therapist would then help her come up with new, constructive ways of relating to her boss.

Q: That sounds a little lopsided. What if the boss is the one who needs therapy?

A: A common criticism of IPT is that it doesn't offer people a critical examination of the social context in which the problem—in this case, the depressive disorder—developed. Applied strictly, IPT won't question whether her boss's demands are appropriate, it will merely seek ways to help her meet them. Of course, if the demands are truly unacceptable, many therapists would advise her to look for another job. But the goal of IPT is to help people do the best they can with what they have.

Q: When is interpersonal therapy most appropriate?

A: According to the American Psychiatric Association, IPT may be most useful for people who are in the midst of recent conflicts with significant others and for those having difficulties adjusting to an altered career or social role or other life transition—for example, someone who is "mourning" the end of a marriage and having trouble coming to terms with being single.

The American Psychological Association's Task Force Report on Women and Depression notes that IPT may be especially helpful for women because relationships are central to a woman's well-being.

It added that this may be even more true for minority women, who tend to define themselves through their personal relationships and run into problems because of their cultural heritage. For example, because Asian American and Hispanic American women are raised to be unassertive, they may need help asserting themselves in relationships.

COGNITIVE/BEHAVIORAL THERAPIES

Q: What's the other main psychotherapeutic approach?

A: As we indicated earlier, the other main approach concentrates on correcting the "faulty" behaviors and ways of thinking that may have led to depression. While insight-oriented psychodynamic therapy tries to help someone learn why she became depressed, these action-oriented therapies focus on specific ways she can change behavior and thinking, right now, to overcome depression.

There are two main therapies: **behavioral therapy** and **cognitive therapy**. Often these are used in combination, as cognitive/behavioral therapy.

Q: Let's take them one at a time. What is behavioral therapy?

A: Behavioral therapy targets specific, observable behaviors—withdrawal, unassertiveness, lack of involvement in enjoyable activities—that are symptoms of a depressive disorder. Then the therapist tries to teach the person how to change her behavior.

Q: What's the depressed person's role in all this?

A: Initially, she might be expected to monitor her activities, moods and thoughts for a period of time, possibly keeping a written record. This provides her and her therapist with an objective baseline from which to measure change and improvement.

It also helps her recognize how certain activities lift her mood while others lower it. "Seeing these relationships on a day-to-day basis impresses on patients in a powerful way the fact that the quantity and the quality of their daily interactions have an important impact on their depression," Peter Lewinsohn, Ph.D., a prominent behavioral psychologist with the Oregon Research Institute, in Eugene, has written. "Patients, in a very real sense, learn to diagnose their own depression."

Q: Where does the treatment go from there?

A: Next she'd set some behavioral goals for herself. The goals should be realistic, to guarantee some early successes. In addition, she'd probably work on changing some specific behaviors that are related to her depression, such as improving her social skills.

To do this, she'd have "homework" assignments. The most important work is actually done between sessions, when the depressed person implements the program. Her therapist may set up behavior "experiments"—tasks that may initially appear daunting. People do these tasks to see if their initial reactions—"I can't do this," "I won't enjoy that"—are valid.

Q: Precisely what are these "daunting" tasks?

A: They're not daredevil activities like mountain climbing. Typically they're social interactions—say, initiating a conversation—that many depressed people are reluctant to undertake.

In fact, the person being treated for depression is encouraged to do things that most people enjoy. For example,

Lewinsohn has developed a "Coping With Depression"
course that employs a "Pleasant Events Schedule" of 320
everyday but enjoyable activities, such as taking a walk or
reading a book. People who take the course rate each item
for enjoyability. That gives them "targets"—activities they
know can lift their spirits when they're moderately depressed.

Q: What are some of the specific tactics taught in
behavioral therapy?

A: There are a number of overlapping behavioral and
cognitive tactics. They can be social skills, to help
improve personal relationships, and coping or "self-
management" skills that help deal with the nitty-gritty
aspects of life rather than be overwhelmed by them. A short
list includes training in assertiveness, relaxation, decision
making, problem solving, communication and time
management.

For example, a person in behavioral therapy might be
taught conversation skills—how to initiate conversations, ask
questions, make appropriate comments and end conversations
gracefully; he may learn "positive" assertion—how to express praise and affection for others, even how to apologize
—and negative assertion (standing up for his rights, com-
municating his own needs).

Q: What do conversation skills and time
management have to do with depression?

A: Because depressed people often have poor social
skills and are uncomfortable and anxious in social
situations, they don't get the positive reinforcement from
interacting with other people that—as we discussed in the
section above on IPT—can be critical to one's moods. If
someone who's depressed can converse more fluently, the

thinking goes, he'll relate more easily to others. If he can express himself, he'll feel less passive and more effective in handling his daily life.

As for time management, Lewinsohn notes that "depressed individuals typically make poor use of their time." By failing to plan ahead—for example, not getting a babysitter—a depressed person may be unable to do something he'd enjoy, like going to the movies. In behavioral therapy, he learns to plan and schedule.

Q: What is relaxation training?

A: Therapists use tools ranging from progressive muscle relaxation and concentrated breathing to guided imagery, in which they suggest images for people to visualize. All of these techniques can help counteract the tension or anxiety that stress or unpleasant situations can produce.

Q: A lot of these techniques sound familiar. Haven't businesses used them to get people to perform better?

A: That's absolutely right. Many of these therapies— time management, relaxation training, assertiveness training (particularly for women)—have a much broader audience than just people who are depressed. Alone or in combination, they've been widely used to motivate people, notably employees, and make them more personally effective and productive.

Q: Is there more to behavioral therapy than these techniques?

A: Yes, it also includes what Lewinsohn calls "environmental interventions," or external changes. These can involve momentous changes, such as moving to another house, taking a job or separating from a spouse. Or they can merely be a matter of a person's therapist changing her family environment, teaching relatives to praise her "adopted" or learned behaviors and to ignore her depressed behaviors.

Q: Changing jobs, ending marriages. Don't those changes just add stress—and cause depression?

A: As we mentioned in Chapter 2, a bad marriage can be a major source of depression, so leaving it can be a positive step. At the same time, taking a job, even if it results short-term in a higher level of stress, can also lift the spirits. As the American Psychological Association Task Force noted, speaking of multiple roles for women, "If things aren't going well in one area, they can compensate by feeling satisfied with their successes in other areas."

Q: All right, let's go on to cognitive therapy. What is it?

A: We'll let Aaron T. Beck, M.D., the founder of cognitive therapy, define it. "Cognitive," says Beck, a psychiatrist who is now director of the Center for Cognitive Therapy at the University of Pennsylvania Medical Center, Philadelphia, refers to "the ways in which people make judgments and decisions, and the ways in which they interpret— or misinterpret—one another's actions. . . . How we think determines to a large extent whether we will succeed and enjoy life, or even survive. If our thinking is straightforward and clear, we are better equipped to reach those goals. If it is bogged down by distorted symbolic meanings, illogical reasoning and erroneous interpretations, we become in effect deaf and blind. "Twisted thinking can be untangled by applying a higher order of reasoning," Beck continues. "We use such high-level thinking much of the time when we catch ourselves in a mistake and correct it."

When someone is depressed, however, she's no longer capable of catching and correcting such mistakes. So the therapist performs that function in cognitive therapy.

Q: Can you give me an example of "twisted thinking" by a person with depressive disorder?

A: In *Love Is Never Enough,* his book about using cognitive therapy to improve relationships, Beck says people with depressive disorder often, on the flimsiest evidence, leap to conclusions and generalizations that reflect badly on themselves. "A depressed wife, for example, may react to her husband's fatigued look with the immediate thought that 'He's sick and tired of me,' " Beck writes.

In another example of "automatic" negative thinking, Beck describes the reaction of a woman to her fiance's silence: Lois jumps to the conclusion that Peter is angry with her, then to the broader idea that he's always angry with her. From there she moves to an even more sweeping generalization—"I always offend people"—and a grim prediction. "The reason I always offend people is because I have no personality. Since I have no personality," Lois concludes, "nobody will ever like me and I will always be lonely."

It's the overgeneralizations—"all-or-nothing words like never, always, all, every and none"—that are particularly common in depressed persons, Beck notes.

Q: What does cognitive therapy do to change this?

A: In a paper Beck co-authored several years ago, he describes the case of Mr. D., a 55-year-old scientist with a 10-year history of chronic depression that periodically flared into major depressive disorder. Mr. D., whose marriage had been troubled for years, had recently become depressed again.

In the first phase of treatment, Mr. D. learned to monitor and record negative thoughts like: "I'm unable to respond to my wife emotionally," "I'm alienated from my family" and, at work, "I have no opinion on anything," "My mind is sluggish . . . I can't speak up at meetings."

"Underlying all of the patient's depressive cognitions," Beck writes, "was the basic formula that if he did not live up to his own idiosyncratic expectations of perfection (which he unquestioningly believed everyone shared), other people 'would not approve' of him." Without such approval, Mr. D. felt, he did not have "the right to exist."

Q: Where did the therapy go from there?

A: Mr. D. was directed to "test out" alternative behaviors and interpretations. For instance, he was told to behave as if his assumption that he needed other people's approval was untrue. Carrying out "assignments" like that allowed him to test his thinking and realize how many of his assumptions bore no relation to reality.

Q: And rethinking is enough to lift depression?

A: Yes, particularly when it's combined with behavioral change. In the initial treatment sessions, Beck has

written, "we often employ behavior techniques such as list-keeping, planning productive activities and scheduling potentially enjoying events. These techniques help to 'break into' the depressive circle." They also serve to distract patients from their depressive thoughts and disprove their belief that they can't do anything or help themselves feel better.

Q: What about follow-up?

A: Sometimes people in cognitive therapy tape their sessions so they can listen to them later. For between-sessions homework, therapists often suggest that patients fill out rating forms and record any recurrent negative thoughts that characterize depressive thinking, as well as details of any difficult encounters with other people.

Patients are urged to make an effort to engage in activities that give them pleasure, and to read about depression and its treatment. Completing these kinds of homework assignments has been shown to play an important role in speeding recovery from depression.

Q: Can you give me specific examples of homework assignments?

A: In a recent article in the *Washington Post,* Tracey Thompson, a journalist who underwent cognitive therapy for depression, listed some of the "assignments" she received:

• "This week, when you feel angry, you have to either note it to yourself or say so immediately."

• "This week, you have to arrange lunch with one person you don't know well but would like to know better."

• "This week, if you catch yourself making any self-serving statement, no matter how trivial, you must stop in the middle of the sentence and correct it immediately."

Q: Are there forms of cognitive therapy other than Beck's?

A: One variation is **rational-emotive therapy (RET)**, developed by psychologist Albert Ellis in 1955. RET is based on the premise that people choose, consciously and unconsciously, how to think and feel. In this view, people create their own emotional problems through illogical thinking, or what Ellis calls irrational beliefs. Regardless of genetics and upbringing, Ellis says, people can consciously choose to change the way they think, so they can resolve their problems by "disputing" those beliefs, or thinking more "scientifically."

Q: Easier said than done. How does it work?

A: In science, Ellis notes, you set up a hypothesis and then check its validity. If it proves false, you reject it and try a new hypothesis. The same procedure takes place in RET.

If you're depressed, you might hypothesize that, because you didn't get the job you wanted, for example, you're unemployable. In therapy, those beliefs would be disputed: Maybe the job interviewer was unfair or inept. Maybe you botched the interview. But that doesn't mean that other interviewers will be unfair or that you'll botch subsequent interviews.

Q: How does someone avoid slipping back into "unscientific" thinking?

A: For RET to be effective, Ellis notes, a person must continually work at changing her beliefs. He suggests that people write down their irrational beliefs and disputes or hold tape-recorded conversations with themselves. Then they and even their friends can go over the notes or tapes to strengthen the way they dispute their irrational beliefs.

If a person is dealing with self-defeating behavior— whether it's indulging in bad habits or refusing to engage in good habits like exercising—Ellis suggests a system of quick penalties (burning a $20 bill) and immediate reinforcement (listening to music).

Q: **What good does a "quick penalty" do?**

A: Ellis says that a stiff penalty is effective because it makes it painful *not* to abandon the self-defeating behavior. "You obviously feel real pain or discomfort when you are trying to break a bad habit," he has written in a book with the beguiling title *How to Stubbornly Refuse to Make Yourself Miserable About Anything—Yes, Anything!* "So pick something even MORE uncomfortable and make yourself do that thing whenever you refuse to give up your harmful habit or whenever you temporarily give it up and then foolishly fall back to it again."

Q: **Who does cognitive therapy help?**

A: According to the American Psychiatric Association, a cognitive approach may best suit people who accept explicit, structured guidance from another person.

OTHER PSYCHOTHERAPIES

Q: **Are there any other kinds of psychotherapy used to treat depression?**

A: One alternative is **feminist psychotherapy**. It's not so much a technique, like behavioral or cognitive therapy, as a philosophy of psychotherapy. Thus it can be interwoven into various forms of psychotherapy, whether psychodynamic or behavioral.

Q: **Okay, so what is the philosophy of feminist psychotherapy?**

A: Feminist psychotherapy takes the view that women's experiences are devalued as a result of the sexism that pervades our culture, and depression is partly a reaction to cultural oppression rather than a biological or psychosocial phenomenon. According to feminist psychotherapy, traditional psychotherapy seeks to define normalcy in terms of male norms, which should not be applied to women.

Q: **What happens in feminist therapy?**

A: More than other therapies, feminist therapy emphasizes empowerment, giving the client or patient a greater sense of self-worth and a voice in the therapy itself. She is the therapist's equal. She is considered to have important expert information about her own problems and solutions; she's encouraged to ask questions and challenge interventions made by the therapist, with whom she's on a first-name basis.

Apart from the style of the therapy, there's also an underlying feminist substance: The person is encouraged to see how sexist social attitudes have shaped her problems.

Q: **So far, you've mentioned only therapies that are one-on-one. Isn't group therapy used for depression?**

A: In fact, there are a few forms of group therapy that may be used to treat depression:

• Marital (or couples) and family therapy, in which marital partners, or parents and children, are seen together by the therapist.

• Group therapy, which is psychotherapy in a group setting—"T-groups," as they were called in the 1970s—that is typically led by a trained therapist.

• Support groups, which emphasize peer self-help and may be leader-led or leaderless.

Q: **Let's look at these separately, starting with family therapy. Why should a person bring in his family if he's the only one who's depressed?**

A: The underlying premise of this type of therapy is that the problem—in this case, the person's depression—is not always limited to just him. It may be symptomatic of a troubled marriage or family; it may in fact be the result of problems in the marriage or family. Unless these issues are addressed in therapy, the thinking goes, his depression will never be fully resolved.

A study of 76 depressed women treated with individual psychotherapy and/or antidepressants, for example, found that those women who entered treatment complaining of marital discord experienced less improvement in their symptoms and were likelier to relapse than women who had no marital disputes when they began treatment. In the view of Demitri F. Papolos, M.D., a New York psychiatrist who has been a leader in family psychoeducation for affective disorder, such findings underscore the need for couples therapy.

Furthermore, even if the depression truly originated within the depressed individual, it's likely that the disorder is affecting the well-being of the spouse or children, as well as the way family members relate to each other and to the person who's depressed.

Q: What's the approach of marriage and family therapy?

A: Again, that depends on the therapist. *The Consumer's Guide to Psychotherapy* says this type of therapy falls into two main categories: the historical perspective and the interactional perspective.

Therapies that have a historical perspective tend to focus on the "story" of the marriage or family: "What are the traditions in your family? How did you get where you are?" The therapist may look at the way the family dynamics force members into certain roles—for example, how a child is required to "entertain" a depressed mother.

Within this perspective, many therapists have a **family systems** orientation. That means they'll want to examine the way family members from the previous generation were cut out of the family network or drawn into a conflict. The therapist will try to establish a family's pattern of interaction, and then teach them how to avoid replicating it in their own lives.

Q: What's an interactional perspective in marriage and family therapy?

A: History is largely disregarded, and the therapist focuses primarily on current behavior patterns of the family, such as poor communication that creates misunderstanding and resentment. Behavioral therapy then may be used to change family interactions.

Q: What happens in a session?

A: While that varies with the therapist's orientation, certain features characterize all family and marital therapy. During the session, for example, the therapist will encourage family members to interact with one another. The patient may be asked to enact a scene. The therapist may be much more of a participant than in individual therapy, but he may also be directive—making observations, dramatizing patterns. Some therapists may become very directive, suggesting that a grown child move out of the house, for example, or that a couple try a separation.

As with cognitive/behavioral therapy, there may be homework. The depressed person may be asked to change places or roles with another family member. She may be asked to put together a tree of her family, tracking influences from one generation to the next. In the next session, she'll review her homework.

Q: What if her spouse or other family members won't come?

A: Some family therapists may refuse to treat a person unless all relevant members attend, at least for the initial evaluation. And even if the therapist will treat her, it may make matters worse if a significant other opts out. For those reasons, it's important to ensure that others are as committed as the patient is before she embarks on family therapy.

Q: Is family therapy short-term?

A: The time frame depends on the therapeutic approach. If the goal is to solve a specific problem by changing specific behaviors, 10 sessions or less may be enough. On the other hand, if the therapist is tackling a problem within the broader context of the family's history and culture, the therapy may be open-ended.

Q: Okay, let's go on to the next category. What's the group-therapy approach?

A: Group therapy can take any of a variety of psycho-therapeutic approaches, from cognitive/behavioral modification to feminism to a more psychodynamic insight orientation. By its nature, however, group therapy empha-sizes cohesiveness and support, sharing of feelings and experiences, feedback about interpersonal skills, and problem solving.

Q: Is group therapy as effective as individual therapy?

A: There haven't been any studies systematically eval-uating the efficacy of various types of individual versus group therapies for people with comparable levels of depression, according to the U.S. Department of Health and Human Services' Depression Guideline Panel.

However, the panel compared group and individual behavioral therapy, and found them equally effective. And Lewinsohn, the behavioralist, says that his "Coping With Depression" course, which is designed as a group treatment, can be effectively used to treat a group of up to 12 depressed people with one teacher/facilitator—not necessarily a certi-fied psychotherapist.

Q: What's the typical makeup of a group?
Would everybody be depressed?

A: On average, groups have about a half-dozen members, chosen by the therapist. The members may have different psychological problems or share the same or similar problems.

The idea is that, even if the members don't have identical problems, just interacting with others enables a person to see himself—his strengths as well as his weaknesses—more accurately. If it is a group with a common problem, he can learn by being with others who are both more and less depressed than he is.

Q: Is group therapy more appropriate for certain types of depression?

A: According to the American Psychiatric Association, group therapy may be particularly helpful for people whose depression is related to bereavement or chronic illness. People benefit from the example of others who've successfully dealt with similar problems, and survivors gain self-esteem by serving as role models for newer patients.

In addition, in the *Consumer's Guide to Psychotherapy,* psychologists Jack Engler and Daniel Goleman state that interpersonal problems are especially well-suited to a group approach.

Q: How do support groups differ from group therapy?

A: Support groups may not have professional leaders, and the emphasis is on peer self-help and consciousness-raising. Members provide support for each other in a setting that encourages them to share feelings and innovative approaches to problems they probably have in common. Typically they're open-ended.

While self-help groups can be extremely valuable, they may also be detrimental if, as is sometimes the case, they discourage members from seeking professional help.

Q: Then who do support groups help?

A: Mental-health experts tend to endorse support groups for specific applications in helping people with depression. For example, the American Psychiatric Association notes that self-help groups may support compliance by people on lifetime medication, such as people with manic depression who are taking **lithium**. The American Psychological Association's Task Force on Women and Depression cites self-help groups for women only.

Support groups can also be an important source of help for the families of people who are depressed.

COMPARISON OF PSYCHOTHERAPIES

Q: Which psychotherapy is most effective in treating depression?

A: There's widespread agreement among mental-health-care professionals that short-term, highly directed therapy—whether psychodynamic or cognitive/behavioral—works best for depression in the so-called acute stage. "The psychotherapy should generally be time-limited, focused on current problems, and aimed at symptom resolution rather than personality change," according to the Depression

Guideline Panel. The panel said time-limited psychotherapy
alone is associated with a better than 50 percent response
rate in patients with mild to moderate major depression.

Even the American Psychological Association, whose
members tend to have a greater bias toward psychodynamic
therapy than do M.D.'s, agrees that the best short-term
therapy for depression is action-oriented. As the Association
puts it, a depressed person needs to know two things:
"What is making me unhappy? What can I do about it?"
When the therapy includes an explicit action plan, such as
journal writing or art therapy, the success rate with depression can go up as much as 80 to 90 percent, according to the
psychologists' association.

Q: What about interpersonal psychotherapy?

A: It also gets high marks for efficacy. The NIMH
Collaborative Study of the Treatment of Depression,
for example, found that IPT eliminated symptoms of depression in about two-thirds of patients who completed a
16-week course.

Q: Does that mean that a more traditional
psychodynamic approach doesn't work?

A: There's not much data on the efficacy of either brief
or long-term psychodynamic psychotherapy for
major depression. However, that doesn't mean that mental-
health professionals have written off psychodynamic therapy.
Many therapists believe that it's critical to include an "insight"
or analytical element, at the very least, when they treat
people with depression.

Q: Is there one kind of psychotherapy that's better for children?

A: Children under the age of eight or nine often have difficulty talking about their experiences or their feelings, so any standard application of the therapies we've discussed may be irrelevant. Often psychotherapists use "play therapy"—using sand, dolls or puppets, toys and games—to allow toddlers to express their feelings and conflicts. Children who are slightly older may draw or model with clay.

Because they're more verbal, children over the age of 9 or 10 can usually handle one of the talk therapies, whether it's psychodynamic or cognitive/behavioral, according to the Children's Hospital of Philadelphia's *Parent's Guide to Childhood and Adolescent Depression.* Because the child's depression may be a reflection of family stress or difficulties, family therapy is usually encouraged.

In addition, group therapy is particularly effective with adolescents because they put such a high value on peer relationships and are more likely to reveal their problems and accept solutions from peers than from adults, according to Lewinsohn and other experts.

Q: In the long run, how effective is psychotherapy for anyone?

A: There's evidence both ways. One study, which was reported recently in the *American Journal of Psychiatry,* found that in a one-year follow-up of 48 patients with major depression who had responded during a 16-week course of cognitive/behavioral therapy, 32 percent relapsed.

Q: Is there recurrence with any psychotherapy?

A: The Depression Guideline Panel says that, to date, there's no proof that psychotherapy in the acute phase prevents recurrence. However, a high recurrence rate could also indicate that the therapy was inappropriate or too brief. The authors of the *American Journal of Psychiatry* article recommend that patients who do not fully recover during the acute treatment phase should be offered either more extended treatment or other types of treatment during follow-up maintenance visits.

Q: What about maintenance treatment to prevent recurrence? Is one psychotherapy better than another?

A: According to the Depression Guideline Panel, maintenance psychotherapy, given at least monthly, does not appear to prevent recurrence, although it may delay the onset of the next episode. But mental-health professionals concede it's hard to measure the effectiveness of psychotherapy, given the variation in therapies, in therapists and in the frequency of psychotherapeutic visits—from once every several months to once or more a week (for active psychotherapy).

In the next chapter, we discuss a number of studies comparing the efficacy of psychotherapy versus medication. The findings are mixed. But in any event, the question of which is more effective may be moot.

Q: Why is that?

A: Because psychotherapy is expensive and there's a national move to drive down spiraling health-care costs. Third-party payers—particularly managed-care companies, such as health maintenance organizations that have their own networks of physicians and psychotherapists—are starting to limit drastically the number of psychotherapy visits they cover. Many are drawing the line at about a half-dozen sessions. People with depressive disorders are finding that it's easier to get insurers to pay for psychopharmaceuticals.

Q: Are insurers dictating the type of treatment, too?

A: To a point. One innovation that is being tried by a growing number of large self-insured employers and managed-care companies is computer-assisted therapy, a method of selecting and measuring treatment by using computer models.

The technology gives therapists the ability to compare the symptoms of their patients who have major depressive disorder with a database of hundreds or thousands of similar cases. They can see how those patients were treated and what the outcomes, or results, were. Are the patients happy? Able to work? Therapists can then tailor their treatments accordingly to get faster results and cut down on visits, which are the most expensive part of care.

Q: Does computer-assisted treatment work?

A: As you might imagine, it's a highly contentious issue within the medical profession. Many professionals maintain that treating mental illness is as much an art as a science, and that databases are too inflexible a measure by which to evaluate and treat someone for depression. Nor do they like someone else dictating the terms of care: If the therapist opposes the recommendations of the computer model, he can expect to be dropped as a provider.

Although there's one study indicating that computer-assisted cognitive therapy was as effective as standard individual cognitive therapy, the field is too new for much statistical evidence either way. The pressure to cut costs, however, suggests that computer-assisted therapy will become more and more common in the future.

Q: Is computer-assisted treatment limited to psychotherapy?

A: No, the models are also set up to help therapists prescribe antidepressants and to change the medication if a patient is not responsive. (The new system is also being applied to other medical conditions and to surgical procedures as well.) But the main focus is psychotherapy. Because of its price tag, employers "are scared of open-ended psychotherapy," Dr. Grayson Norquist, associate director of services research at the NIMH, told the *New York Times.*

5 MEDICATION

Q: What is an antidepressant?

A: It's a medication that prevents or relieves depression. It helps the brains of people who are depressed to produce neurochemicals they may be missing. A different type of medication, discussed toward the end of this chapter, is prescribed for people with manic depression.

Q: Aren't these drugs pretty controversial?

A: Yes. Unfortunately, there's still a stigma attached to the use of medications for mental illness, just as there remains a stigma to mental illness itself. A Gallup poll in 1993 found that 25 percent of the general public would refuse an antidepressant.

At the same time, however, there's been a substantial increase in the number of people taking antidepressants, particularly Prozac, a drug discussed in detail later in this chapter. Since it was introduced in 1988, Prozac has been used by 6 million people in the United States, 11 million worldwide.

Q: Aren't groups like Alcoholics Anonymous opposed to antidepressants?

A: Not at all. AA is neutral on the subject. Officials state that the organization has no policy on the use of medications for mental illness.

However, many AA members seem to regard the use of psychopharmaceuticals as a violation of the 12-step recovery program. "Some of my recovery brothers and sisters maintain that a person on psychiatric drugs is not 'clean and sober,' " a lawyer who takes antidepressants wrote in an essay in *Newsweek* recently.

The lawyer, who lives in Denver, noted that this philosophy is reinforced by social agencies; most halfway houses in her city accept recovering alcoholics and addicts but turn away people taking psychiatric medications.

Q: I suppose there are several kinds of antidepressants?

A: There are three main categories of antidepressants, which we discuss in detail later in this chapter:

- **Tricyclics (TCAs)**
- **Monoamine oxidase inhibitors (MAOIs)**
- **Selective serotonin reuptake inhibitors (SSRIs)**

There are also a few antidepressants that are chemically unrelated to these groups. And there are still other medications —notably lithium—that are not antidepressants but are used to treat people with manic depression and other disorders.

Q: Which of the antidepressants is best?

A: Surprisingly, perhaps, they're rated about equal in combating depression. After reviewing more than

400 clinical trials of antidepressants, the Depression Guideline Panel concluded that "no one antidepressant is clearly more effective than another. No single medication results in remission for all patients." And it listed several different medications, which we'll discuss below, that might be tried first to treat depression.

Q: Then how does a doctor know which drug to prescribe for someone with major depressive disorder?

A: Unfortunately, there's no sure way of knowing beforehand which medication will be effective. Scientists have been trying to develop biochemical tests that predict how patients with depression will respond to treatment, but so far they've been unsuccessful. As a result, antidepressant therapy is partly a matter of trial and error. Only 50 to 60 percent of patients respond to the first drug they try. A depressed person's doctor may have to prescribe a few antidepressants —not only one from each category, but a couple within a category—before finding the most effective.

Q: So choosing an antidepressant is purely guesswork?

A: No, it's not that uncertain. Because certain depressive conditions generally respond better to particular antidepressants, the doctor should take into consideration the type of disorder the depressed person has. She should also consider the side effects of the various drugs. If the person has insomnia, for example, the doctor may prescribe a sedating drug, such as trazodone or one of the TCAs. If the patient has successfully used a specific antidepressant for a previous depression, there's a good chance he'll get that prescription refilled.

Q: Can someone take more than one type of antidepressant at a time?

A: Yes, and that's sometimes recommended. Some patients whose depression is particularly resistant to treatment may benefit from combination therapy, such as a TCA plus MAOI, lithium plus MAOI or an antidepressant plus a thyroid supplement.

Q: Why a thyroid supplement?

A: For reasons not entirely clear, thyroid-hormone levels can have an impact on the effectiveness of an antidepressant. "A depressed person whose thyroid gland is the slightest bit underactive will respond poorly to antidepressants," Francis M. Mondimore, M.D., a psychiatrist with the Carolina Medical Center for Mental Health in Charlotte, North Carolina, has written in *Depression: The Mood Disease.* "Even if the thyroid-hormone level seems normal, adding a small dose of thyroid medication seems to boost the effect of the antidepressants and turn an incomplete response into a complete remission of symptoms."

Q: So it's always safe to combine antidepressants?

A: No, certain antidepressants have dangerous interactions when taken together. For example, TCAs can interact with MAOIs to produce fever, agitation, convulsions and even death. If they are used together, professionals say, the MAOI should be added to the TCA, and lower doses of both drugs should be used initially.

Combining an SSRI and an MAOI has been known to produce a number of symptoms—chills, fever, skin rash, lymph-node enlargement, fatigue—and, in the worst-case scenario, precipitate a "serotonergic crisis," characterized by high fever (often over 104 °F.), rapid heartbeat, falling blood pressure and coma. In some cases this has led to death.

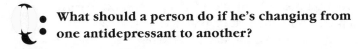

What should a person do if he's changing from one antidepressant to another?

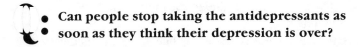

In some cases—switching from a TCA, for example, to paroxetine—he can make the transition immediately. In other cases, he'll have to observe a "washout" period to get one drug out of his system before introducing another. His physician should advise him.

Usually a two-week wait is adequate when switching from an MAOI to a TCA or SSRI, vice versa, or from one MAOI to another, or from one SSRI to another. In still other circumstances—switching from fluoxetine to an MAOI, or from an MAOI to the tricyclic clomipramine (Anafranil, made by Ciba-Geigy)—the medical profession recommends a washout period of five to six weeks.

Can people stop taking the antidepressants as soon as they think their depression is over?

It's dangerous to stop taking antidepressants abruptly. Stopping prematurely could cause a relapse and, even if a depressive episode has ended, the body has become accustomed to a certain dosage. Patients should discontinue medication as they took it, under a physician's care.

Q: What about preventing a recurrence of depression? Is one antidepressant more effective than the others?

A: There's no clear evidence that one is better than another, particularly given the newness of the SSRIs.
   A five-year study by researchers at the University of Pittsburgh School of Medicine, of 128 people with recurrent depression, found that imipramine, a TCA, was highly effective in preventing subsequent episodes. Similarly, a separate study of people with recurrent depression found that 39 percent of those treated with a placebo suffered a new episode of depression during the course of a year, compared to only 15 percent of those treated with paroxetine, an SSRI.

Q: Is there anyone who shouldn't take any of the antidepressants?

A: There's been some suggestion that antidepressants may not be effective—at least in their usual dosages —for women taking tamoxifen, which is widely used as a treatment for breast cancer and is also being studied as a means of preventing breast cancer. One theory is that the drugs lose their impact due to the increase in MAO in these women.
   Other medications, including beta blockers (medications used primarily to control high blood pressure, tremors and migraines) and arthritis drugs, may render antidepressants or antimania drugs less effective.

Q: Is it all right for children to take antidepressants?

A: Although psychotherapy is the preferred treatment, medication is sometimes prescribed for children who are depressed. Contradictory data exist about the efficacy of antidepressants for children before puberty. Some studies have shown that children respond to the tricyclic imipramine, while other studies indicate that tricyclics are no more effective than placebos. As for safety, there are no data on long-term effects, because antidepressants have been prescribed for children for only the past 10 to 15 years.

Q: **When antidepressants are prescribed for children, what's the usual protocol?**

A: TCAs are usually the first drugs used, because they have the longest track record. The SSRIs, however, are becoming increasingly popular. In both cases, the dosage is adjusted for body weight. MAOIs are rarely prescribed because they require rigid dietary restrictions that children may have trouble following.

Q: **Any special rules or prohibitions for the elderly?**

A: As we noted, because older people may have other medical conditions and be taking numerous other drugs, they—or their physicians—must be alert to possible complications. That aside, they can be treated with the same range of antidepressants. But it's noteworthy that they don't tolerate higher doses as well as younger people and need a longer period of adjustment between changes in dosages. For physicians who prescribe antidepressants for the elderly, the rule is, "Start low and go slow."

TRICYCLICS

Q: Let's take the antidepressants one by one. What are tricyclics?

A: Tricyclic antidepressants, widely known as TCAs— the name derives from the drug's triple-carbon-ring chemical structure—have been prescribed since the 1950s for depression and, until recently, were the clear first choice of physicians for the vast majority of people with major depressive disorder.

You might recognize this category better by some of its generic or brand names: imipramine (Tofranil, manufactured by Ciba-Geigy), amitriptyline (Elavil, made by Roche Laboratories) and nortriptyline (Pamelor, by Sandoz Pharmaceuticals).

Q: How do they work?

A: TCAs raise the levels of serotonin and norepinephrine in the brain by slowing the rate of **reuptake**, or reabsorption, by nerve cells. It may take several weeks for levels to reach a point where the symptoms of depression disappear.

Q: Are there side effects?

A: Because TCAs, to varying degrees, also block other neurotransmitters, they have a number of possible side effects. These vary with the specific medication taken and the individual. One TCA may make people feel drowsy while another may have little effect and even produce feelings of anxiety or restlessness.

In general, tricyclics tend to produce **anticholinergic** side effects, because they block cholinergic receptors in the brain. The most common side effects are dry mouth (85 percent of subjects, in one study), constipation (one-third of the group, in the same study) and urinary retention, or difficulty urinating. Other anticholinergic effects, particularly in the elderly, can include cognitive and memory difficulties.

Other common side effects include weight gain, increased sweating (24 percent in the study), dizziness (20 percent), decrease in sexual ability and desire, muscle twitches, fatigue, weakness and nausea. Some people find their hearts beat far more rapidly and, in rare cases, they may develop irregular heart rhythms.

These side effects often disappear quickly or can be reduced by lowering the dosage or changing to another tricyclic.

Q: Are there real dangers associated with TCAs?

A: Because they can cause serious cardiac complications, TCAs can be lethal if misused at high doses. According to Eliot Gelwan, a psychopharmacologist who lectures in psychiatry at Harvard Medical School, TCAs are the leading cause of death by drug overdose in the United States. Because people with major depressive disorder may be contemplating suicide, the danger of overdosing must be taken into account by any doctor prescribing TCAs.

Q: Who should take TCAs?

A: Tricyclics are still preferred by many physicians because they have a far longer history and therefore are more of a known quantity than the up-and-coming category of antidepressant, the SSRI. In evaluating all the antidepressants, the Depression Guideline Panel named TCAs like nortriptyline and desipramine (Norpramin, made by Marion Merrell Dow) among the drugs they'd try first.

As for specific groups, TCAs may be the most appropriate antidepressants—or the least potentially harmful—for women who are pregnant, particularly in the second and third trimesters, according to Jane Summers, M.D., a psychiatrist who treats postpartum depression patients at Pennsylvania Hospital in Philadelphia. While SSRIs may be equally safe, Summers notes, they're so new that there's no significant record of their effect on fetal development.

However, the *Physicians' Desk Reference,* a reference guide to pharmaceuticals that is consulted by most members of the medical community, says that even TCAs should be used "only if the clinical condition clearly justifies potential risk to the fetus." And because the drug passes into breast milk, a new mother shouldn't nurse if she's taking a tricyclic or other antidepressant.

Q: Are there people who shouldn't take TCAs?

A: Because TCAs may create cardiovascular problems, people with a history of heart disease should avoid them. They may also want to avoid TCAs if they're on any of a number of drugs with which TCAs interact dangerously: thyroid supplements, antihypertensive medications, oral contraceptives, some blood coagulants, some sleeping medications, antipsychotic drugs (such as Thorazine and Haldol, used to treat psychosis, including psychotic depression and severe mania), **diuretics**, antihistamines and aspirin, as well as bicarbonate of soda, vitamin C, alcohol and tobacco.

Other people who may have problems with TCAs are soft-contact-lens wearers. The anticholinergic effect of decreased tearing may lead to excessive deposits of thick mucoid secretions on the lenses, which cause the eyes to itch.

MONOAMINE OXIDASE INHIBITORS (MAOIs)

Q: What are MAOIs?

A: Drugs that inhibit monoamine oxidase, an enzyme that is found in many parts of the body. In the brain, monoamine oxidase destroys neurotransmitters, such as norepinephrine and serotonin. So MAO inhibitors, by limiting the activity of monoamine oxidase, block the breakdown of those neurotransmitters.

Three leading MAOIs are phenelzine (Nardil, made by Parke-Davis), tranylcypromine (Parnate, from SmithKline Beecham) and isocarboxazid (Marplan, made by Roche).

Q: Who should take MAOIs?

A: Traditionally, MAOIs have been prescribed for people who don't respond to the tricyclics. They're also commonly prescribed for cases of atypical depression, a disorder that—as we describe in Chapter 1—presents the direct opposite of the typical symptoms of depression.

In addition, some research suggests that, perhaps because they have a stimulating rather than sedating effect, they may be preferable to TCAs for treating dysthymia, which you'll remember is a chronic, low-level depression.

Q: What are the side effects of MAOIs?

A: MAOIs may cause some side effects similar to those of certain other antidepressants, including dizziness, rapid heartbeat and loss of sexual interest.

One peculiarity of MAOIs is that they react with certain foods and alcoholic beverages, as well as some medications, to produce a severe reaction. The reaction, which often does not appear for several hours after taking the medication, may include a dangerous rise in blood pressure, as well as headache, nausea, vomiting, rapid heartbeat, possible confusion, psychotic symptoms, seizures, stroke and coma.

Q: What foods and drinks are restricted?

A: It's a rather odd grocery list. It includes aged cheeses; smoked, pickled, fermented and otherwise processed meats, fish and soy products; Chianti and other red wines; fava beans and ripe figs; and foods containing monosodium glutamate (MSG). What they have in common is that they contain large amounts of the amino acid tyramine, which, when it interacts with MAOIs, dramatically raises blood pressure.

Drugs with which MAOIs may interact include some over-the-counter cold and allergy medicines and appetite suppressants, local anesthetics, insulin, medicines used to treat Parkinson's disease, amphetamines and cocaine.

Q: So what's a person to do?

A: If someone does take MAOIs, she should be sure to have a complete list of all foods, beverages and other medications to avoid.

SELECTIVE SEROTONIN REUPTAKE INHIBITORS (SSRIs)

Q: What's a selective serotonin reuptake inhibitor?

A: SSRIs, the newest of the three main categories of anti-depressants, are a group of drugs that treat depression by "selectively" inhibiting the reuptake of serotonin. That means that, unlike TCAs, they are unlikely to block the cholinergic receptors in the brain.

While you may not have heard of SSRIs, you might be familiar with the first of the SSRIs to become available in the United States: Prozac (fluoxetine), manufactured by Eli Lilly. Other drugs in this category include sertraline (Zoloft, manufactured by Pfizer) and paroxetine (Paxil, manufactured by SmithKline Beecham).

Q: Why have I been hearing so much about Prozac?

A: It's the most commonly prescribed antidepressant in the United States and the world. And it's had a lot of publicity, good and bad.

In 1990, two years after it was introduced in the United States, *Newsweek* actually featured Prozac on the cover under the headline "a breakthrough drug for depression."

It's been widely acclaimed because it treats depression without the adverse effects of other antidepressants, such as the dry mouth caused by TCAs or the dietary restrictions mandated by MAOIs.

Q: What was the negative publicity?

A: A few years ago, Prozac became the target of the
Church of Scientology, a group whose goal, stated in
a report in 1991 on CBS's "60 Minutes," is to "remove psychiatry completely from the world and to put Scientology in
its place as the foremost mental-health therapy." The Scien-
tologists launched a multimillion-dollar campaign against
Prozac, accusing it of causing people to become suicidal and
commit murder.

In 1990 the Citizens Commission on Human Rights, a
group founded by the Church of Scientology, asked the Food
and Drug Administration to remove Prozac from the market.
The FDA refused.

Q: What evidence was there that Prozac was harmful?

A: In 1989 a man in Louisville, Kentucky, went on a ram-
page, gunning down eight coworkers before killing
himself. An autopsy revealed that he had been taking Prozac.

Then in February 1990, the *American Journal of Psychiatry* published an article by Martin Teicher, M.D., a Harvard
psychiatrist, about six patients who had had suicidal thoughts
while taking Prozac. When they stopped taking Prozac, their
suicidal thoughts disappeared.

Q: Doesn't that suggest that Prozac is dangerous?

A: As Teicher himself has been the first to note, the
connection isn't clear. The six patients had unusually
complicated and enduring forms of depression, most of them
were also taking other drugs that could also have affected

their mood or behavior, and three of them had tried previously to commit suicide. Teicher notes that he has continued to prescribe Prozac for people with depression.

Then is Prozac completely safe?

A: Prozac has been known to trigger manic episodes in people with a personal and/or family history of bipolar disorder, but that's also true of other categories of antidepressants.

The Depression Guideline Panel lists Prozac, Paxil and Zoloft among the handful of drugs to be tried early on in treating depression. If physicians sound a cautionary note about SSRIs these days, it's partly because they have a short history and partly because—like all antidepressants—they have side effects.

What are the side effects?

A: Gastrointestinal distress (nausea and diarrhea), anxiety or nervousness, insomnia, headache and rash have all been associated with initial doses of Prozac as well as the other SSRIs. Unlike some other antidepressants, which can lead to weight gain, the SSRIs can sometimes cause a slight weight loss.

Precisely how common these side effects are depends on the specific SSRI. As an example, however, we'll note that a couple of studies associated paroxetine (Paxil) with anxiety in 13.5 percent of all subjects and vomiting in 15 percent of elderly patients.

In addition, more than 10 percent of men taking SSRIs have also developed impotence problems, and a small percentage of both men and women may lose interest in sex or become slow or unable to achieve orgasm. That's a complication that occurs with virtually any antidepressant, but it seems to be most common with Prozac and the MAOIs.

Q: Who should take the SSRIs?

A: SSRIs are often prescribed for the elderly because, according to some studies, older people can tolerate the same starting dose as given to much younger people and because the SSRIs have a reputation for relatively mild side effects. For example, they're less likely to cause low blood pressure, which may lead to falls. On the other hand, the elderly may be unable to tolerate the gastrointestinal side effects.

One study found marked improvement in depressed post-menopausal women who took Prozac together with estrogen-replacement therapy. And, because of their side-effect profile, SSRIs are often prescribed for people with cardio-vascular illness.

Q: But I've heard Prozac described as a miracle drug for just about anybody with a mental illness—or even a personality quirk.

A: It has acquired a reputation for helping people over-come not only their basic depressive symptoms but other conditions, ranging from overeating to obsessive-compulsive disorder. It's also been reported to help people overcome problems that were traditionally thought to require psychotherapy: excessive sensitivity to criticism, fear of rejection, lack of self-esteem and a limited ability to expe-rience pleasure.

In *Listening to Prozac,* a book about this phenomenon, author Peter D. Kramer describes patients, already successful

and healthy individuals, who bloomed with the help of
Prozac. The drug, one of his patients told him, made people
"better than well."

Q: Does it really do that?

A: The evidence at this point is mostly anecdotal, as re-
searchers say—that is, it's one patient's or physician's
word against another's. Philip Gold, M.D., a research psychiatrist and chief of NIMH's neuroendocrinology branch, rejects
the notion that antidepressants can or should be used merely
to improve one's personality. People who are on an even keel
"do not respond to these agents." He observed in a 1994
article in *Atlantic Monthly,* "The idea that healthy people
who take Prozac feel better is absolutely ridiculous."

OTHER ANTIDEPRESSANTS

Q: You said there are a few other types of antidepressants that don't fit into the three main categories. What are they?

A: As of this writing, the major ones are venlafaxine
(Effexor, manufactured by Wyeth-Ayerst Laboratories),
trazodone (Desyrel, made by Mead Johnson Pharmaceuticals)
and a relatively new antidepressant, buproprion (Wellbutrin,
manufactured by Burroughs Wellcome). New antidepressants
are being developed continuously, and more may be coming
onto the market soon.

Q: What are these other antidepressants like?

A: Effexor resembles the SSRIs, although it inhibits reuptake of both norepinephrine and serotonin. Trazodone also inhibits serotonin reuptake, but it's chemically different from the SSRIs.

Buproprion is a bit of a mystery, because scientists don't completely understand how it works. However, it's believed that it inhibits the reuptake of dopamine as well as serotonin and norepinephrine.

Q: What are their pros and cons?

A: Effexor has some of the same relatively mild side effects of TCAs and SSRIs. In drug trials, a small percentage of people stopped taking Effexor because of nausea, sleepiness or dizziness.

Trazodone causes fewer side effects, such as cardiac difficulties, than the TCAs. Because it's extremely sedating, it's more appropriate for people whose depressive symptoms include agitation. One major drawback is that it's been known to cause priapism, or a painful, prolonged erection, that, in about one-third of the cases reported, has required surgical intervention.

Q: And buproprion?

A: Shortly after being introduced several years ago, Buproprion was taken off the market because it was believed to cause seizures. It was recently reintroduced after it was found that the seizures tended to occur only with people who are bulimic, have had head trauma or have a personal or family history of seizure disorders. The more common side effects include agitation, headache, nausea, vomiting, constipation, tremor and dry mouth.

Buproprion doesn't have the TCAs' sedating effect—in fact, it's been associated with insomnia—and it's been prescribed for people who don't respond to TCAs. According to the NIMH, it's tolerated well by people who have recurrent depressions with hypomania (mild manic depression).

Q: Are there any other medications to treat depression?

A: Sometimes older depressed people who don't respond to conventional antidepressants are given medications that are central-nervous-system stimulants, such as methylphenidate (Ritalin, made by Ciba-Geigy). These drugs don't lift the depression but they may improve symptoms. The U.S. Health and Human Services' Depression Guideline Panel has given such medications a cautious endorsement, with the proviso that patients undergo clinical **psychopharmacology** before they start taking one.

TREATMENT FOR MANIC DEPRESSION

Q: What's the primary medication for manic depression?

A: People with manic-depressive disorder have traditionally been given some form of the element lithium, a natural saltlike sodium that seems to even out mood swings in both directions. In fact, for decades lithium was virtually the only treatment for manic depression. Some of the brand

names under which lithium is sold are Lithane (Miles Pharmaceuticals), Eskalith (made by SmithKline Beecham) and
Lithobid and Cibalith (Ciba-Geigy).

However, lithium is effective for only about half the people
who've tried it, and these days a couple of other medications
—products normally used to treat epilepsy—are widely used
to control manic depression.

Q: So for someone who's manic depressive, she
just takes lithium or these antiepileptic drugs
every day?

A: It's not quite that simple. If a person is diagnosed
during the onset of a manic phase, she might be
given not only lithium but an antipsychotic medication, such
as haloperidol (Haldol, made by McNeil Pharmaceutical) or
chlorpromazine (Thorazine, from SmithKline Beecham) until
the lithium can take effect. It can take 5 to 14 days to
diminish severe manic symptoms.

Alternatively, during depressive phases, her doctor might
prescribe short-term treatment with an antidepressant. Sometimes, however, this backfires, precipitating manic episodes
or increasing the frequency of mood swings.

Q: How does lithium work?

A: It has several biological effects throughout the body,
but how it works against manic depression isn't
understood, particularly since it is effective against both
depression and mania.

Q: **Since it's used for mania, does it have a sedating effect?**

A: It doesn't sedate or even affect your normal energy levels, but some people complain that it makes them feel groggy, and Charles L. Bowden, M.D., a psychiatrist at the University of Texas Health Science Center at San Antonio, says that about one-third of people who take lithium suffer some memory impairment.

Q: **You said earlier that there's a strong connection between manic depression and creativity. Does lithium suppress creativity?**

A: There's conflicting anecdotal evidence about lithium's effect on a person's "special spark." Some, like actress Patty Duke, believe it's only beneficial. In *A Brilliant Madness,* she wrote, lithium "keeps me even. . . . That, together with the therapy I needed to mop up the debris in my life, made all the difference."

On the other hand, the poet Robert Lowell once told the neurologist Oliver Sacks about being on lithium for his manic-depressive disorder, "I feel much 'better,' in a way, calmer, stabler—but my poetry has lost much of its force."

Q: **Are there other side effects?**

A: There are a number of side effects that occur in perhaps 40 percent of people taking lithium.

Early side effects include gastrointestinal symptoms (nausea, vomiting, diarrhea), hand tremor, muscle weakness and increased thirst and urination. These, along with fatigue or drowsiness, usually disappear or subside quickly. However, some people continue to have hand tremors. Some even gain weight.

Because lithium is almost entirely eliminated from the body by the kidneys, a person may also develop kidney changes, but these are generally managed by lowering the dosage of lithium; unmanaged, they can lead to renal failure. In addition, lithium may cause the thyroid gland to become underactive or enlarged. A doctor should monitor the thyroid function of someone taking lithium and, if necessary, prescribe thyroid hormone along with the lithium.

Q: Are lithium dosages determined like antidepressants—trial and error?

A: No, blood tests are used to determine the correct dosage for any individual. When someone starts medication, her doctor will initially check the level of lithium in her blood every few days. Too little lithium is ineffective, too much is toxic, and the range between an effective dose and a dangerous one is relatively small. Once she's stable and on a maintenance dosage, her lithium level should be checked every few months.

Q: How long would someone have to be on lithium?

A: Because cycles of manic depression tend to occur at frequent intervals, many people who have manic-depressive disorder are on lithium for life. Since the disorder typically strikes young people, treatment may start when they're in their teens. Other people have episodes that are so minor or far apart that lifetime therapy isn't necessary.

If a patient does go off lithium, however, physicians say she should taper off the drug gradually. Stopping abruptly can trigger the kind of manic episode described by Kate Millett in *The Loony Bin Trip*. Although Millett later withdrew successfully from lithium after taking it for seven years, she did so over the course of six months. Furthermore, for reasons that are unclear, if someone stops lithium suddenly, the drug may not work if or when she needs to take it again.

Q: **If a person is on lithium for a lifetime, does she have to watch her diet the way she would with, say, MAOIs?**

A: Although lithium may lead to a weight gain, crash diets are a bad idea because they may affect the lithium level. Unfortunately, a person taking lithium may even be precluded from an otherwise healthful low-salt diet. The reason is that anything that lowers the level of sodium in the body may cause a lithium buildup and lead to toxicity. Obviously, a reduced salt intake could do that; so could heavy sweating, fever, vomiting or diarrhea.

Q: **What about other medications? Is there a need to be careful?**

A: Yes. Lithium can interact badly with some other medications, including several antibiotics, such as tetracycline and Flagyl, and certain anti-inflammatory agents, including aspirin and ibuprofen (Motrin, Advil, Nuprin are prominent brand names). If it's only a painkiller that's needed, the person should take an acetaminophen product like Tylenol. While some diuretics can raise lithium levels, others—like coffee and tea—can lower the level. If someone is on lithium, she should tell all her doctors and even her dentist.

Q: You said high levels of lithium can be toxic. What happens?

A: A person developing lithium toxicity—also known as lithium poisoning or intoxication—may become nauseated, drowsy, confused and dizzy; she may also experience mental dullness, slurred speech, confusion, dizziness, muscle twitching, irregular heartbeat and blurred vision. A serious lithium overdose can be fatal.

Q: Basically, though, lithium is safe?

A: Yes, if levels are monitored regularly, according to the psychiatric community. Patty Duke writes that her personal warning signal is a metallic taste in her mouth; when it comes on, she goes to her doctor for tests, which generally result in a lowering of her dosage.

However, because of possible complications, lithium may not be recommended when a person has existing thyroid, kidney or heart disorders, epilepsy or brain damage. In addition, lithium increases the risk of congenital malformations in babies born to women taking lithium. The medical community warns against the use of lithium specifically during the first three months of pregnancy.

Q: What medications can be taken instead of lithium?

A: Often people with manic depression who don't respond to lithium are given an anticonvulsant medication—a drug designed to suppress seizures—such as carbamazepine (Tegretol, manufactured by Ciba-Geigy) and valproate (Depakote, made by Abbott Laboratories). These seem to be particularly effective for people whose manic depression takes the form of mixed mood disorder (intense depression and mania at the same time) or rapid cycling (four or more mood episodes per year).

As of this writing, neither of those anticonvulsants has received FDA approval for manic depression. However, since they're available, a doctor can prescribe them for her patients. Some people take one of the anticonvulsants as well as lithium.

Q: Do they have side effects?

A: Both carbamazepine and valproate may initially make someone drowsy and clumsy; carbamazepine may cause blurring of vision and skin rashes, and valproate can cause skin and hair changes, nausea, vomiting and indigestion. These effects tend to be mild and short-lived, and can be managed in part by temporarily reducing the dosage or taking the drug with food.

In addition, each medication has potentially more serious side effects. In rare cases, both drugs can lead to hepatitis. Another possible complication of carbamazepine is aplastic anemia, in which the bone marrow is compromised in its ability to manufacture new blood cells. Because of these risks, periodic blood tests are needed as long as the person is taking these medications.

6 MORE ON TREATMENTS

Q: You've talked at length about the two major treatments for depression: psychotherapy and medication. Are there any other approaches?

A: There are a few other major treatments: electro-convulsive therapy, light therapy and, as a general category, alternative treatments. We'll discuss each of these in turn, and then compare and contrast the major therapies.

ELECTROCONVULSIVE THERAPY

Q: What is electroconvulsive therapy (ECT)? Is that the same as shock therapy?

A: ECT is a treatment for severe mood disorders in which a low-voltage current is sent to the brain—through electrodes placed either on both sides or on one side of the scalp—for about two seconds, to induce a generalized seizure or convulsion. Doctors prefer to call it electroconvulsive therapy since it's the convulsion, not the shock, that helps alleviate depression.

Q: How exactly does it help alleviate depression?

A: Scientists know that ECT temporarily obliterates the normal electrical patterns of the brain. They've also established that ECT alters the receptors for the same group of neurotransmitters that tricyclic antidepressants affect. Beyond that, though, how ECT works to treat depression is still a mystery.

Q: Doesn't it hurt?

A: It did at one time, when it was performed without anesthesia or muscle relaxants. During seizures, people underwent such violent muscle spasms that many lost teeth or suffered complications like vertebral compression fractures; 1 in 1,000 died as a result of the treatment.

These days, however, people are briefly put to sleep with an intravenous anesthetic; they also receive a relaxant to minimize muscular response during the treatment. When they awaken, they're likely to be temporarily confused and headachy, and about 10 percent are also agitated, but they're not in pain.

Q: I thought nobody used ECT anymore. How common is it?

A: Until a decade or so ago, ECT had been largely discredited as a treatment for depression. Part of the reason was its unsavory past: In the United States in the 1940s and 1950s, ECT was a new technique that was often administered to the most severely disturbed patients in large mental institutions for a variety of disorders, frequently in high doses and for long periods. The 1975 movie *One Flew*

Over the Cuckoo's Nest confirmed many people's view that
ECT was given, as the American Psychiatric Association
recently observed, "even to control troublesome patients."

In the past decade, however, ECT has made a comeback.
The NIMH has estimated that 110,000 people each year receive
ECT. And while most people are still reluctant to admit
they've had the procedure, even that is starting to change;
not long ago Dick Cavett, the talk-show host, spoke publicly
about his successful treatment with ECT for depression.

Q: But isn't it still pretty controversial?

A: Yes, it's one of the most controversial treatments in
psychiatry. The main reason is ECT's long-term
impact on memory.

After ECT, most people have short-term memory loss,
usually **retrograde amnesia**—a failure to recall events
within a few months before and after the treatment. Some
people may also find that their ability to learn and retain
new information, which is the most vital aspect of memory,
may be impaired for several weeks. Most people recover their
memories, but some do not. According to the American
Psychiatric Association, 1 patient in 200 reports severe
memory problems that remain for months or even years.
Some people say that, while ECT improved their depressive
symptoms, it devastated their lives.

Q: That sounds terrible. So what's the case for ECT?

A: In its defense, some psychiatrists argue that, because
severely depressed individuals often have memory
and cognitive problems, it can be hard to distinguish between
memory loss induced by ECT and loss caused by depression.

And they point to patients like the late Vladimir Horowitz, the great concert pianist, whose memory was conspicuously unimpaired by ECT.

The bottom line, of course, is that electroconvulsive therapy evidently does help lift the most severe depressions. A recent study by Harold A. Sackeim, Ph.D., a psychologist who is chief of biological psychiatry at the New York State Psychiatric Institute, Manhattan, found that 79 percent of patients ultimately responded to ECT after other methods, including medication, had failed. "ECT is the most effective treatment we have for severe depression," Sackeim says.

Q: Why is there so much variation in memory loss?

A: That's hard to say. None of the studies has shown evidence that ECT actually destroys brain tissue. But side effects, including memory loss, seem to be more severe when the seizures last longer, the treatments are more frequent and numerous, and there's a higher dosage of electrical stimulation.

Research also indicates that ECT produces less confusion and memory loss when electrodes are placed unilaterally, on the "nondominant" side of the brain, instead of the traditional bilateral placement. However, there's also some evidence that unilateral placement may be less effective or require more treatments. Scientists are experimenting with different placements for the electrodes. In the meantime, the American Psychiatric Association has recommended that electrode placement be decided on a case-by-case basis.

Q: How many treatments are usually given?

A: People typically receive 8 to 12 sessions over three weeks.

Q: Who should have ECT?

A: In 1985 a consensus panel of the NIMH agreed that the best candidates for ECT are people with delusional and melancholic depressions. They also said ECT is as effective as lithium for people in the acute manic phase. Other forms of depression, including dysthymia, have been ruled out for ECT.

At the same time, the panel widened the list of candidates who could benefit from ECT to include people who have failed to respond to antidepressants and people whose medical conditions preclude the use of antidepressants—a category that includes many elderly people, as well as women with psychotic depression during the first trimester of pregnancy.

The panel added that ECT should be considered for someone who is at immediate risk of suicide because of depression, or risks serious medical complications or death through exhaustion because of mania. "The severe and unremitting nature of the patient's emotional suffering, or extreme incapacitation, are also important considerations," the panel said.

Q: So it's the more extreme cases that qualify for treatment?

A: Yes. The 1985 consensus statement still prevails, although there's growing interest in expanding the application of ECT. In response to the Sackeim study, a couple of researchers from NIMH wrote in the *New England Journal of Medicine* that "these new results challenge the common practice of subjecting suffering patients to months of futile medication trials; in our opinion, electroconvulsive therapy should be offered as a reasonable choice earlier in the treatment process."

Q: Don't older people often have ECT?

A: Yes, partly because of medical problems that preclude the use of antidepressants. According to Peter Breggin, director of the Center for the Study of Psychiatry, Bethesda, Maryland, most of the people who receive ECT are elderly women. Breggin, who has called for a ban on the use of ECT, calculates that in 1988 in California—a state that requires reporting of every ECT treatment—53 percent of ECT patients were 65 years or older.

Q: Does it affect older people differently?

A: A recent study confirmed that older patients, particularly those over 80, often become delirious immediately after ECT but said it doesn't endanger them. In 1990 the American Psychiatric Association strongly supported ECT for the elderly, but it acknowledged that the aged suffer "an increased likelihood of appreciable memory deficits and confusion during the course of the treatment." The report also noted that it is harder to cause a convulsion in the elderly, so more electrical current must be used.

Q: That sounds like it would put people at risk. Does it?

A: The stronger electrical stimulus and the lower-dose anesthetic used in older patients may expose them to more ECT-induced cardiovascular stress, according to one recent study, which urged serious reexamination of the practice, especially for geriatric patients. But another study, of 193 elderly patients with depression, found that ECT had no effect on mortality rates.

Q: Is there anyone who absolutely shouldn't have ECT?

A: There are a number of people whose medical conditions preclude ECT. Those conditions are serious cardiovascular disease, such as angina or a recent history of heart attacks; abnormalities of the blood vessels that may cause them to rupture easily, such as aneurysms in the brain or aorta; and increased pressure in the brain caused by tumors, blood clots or excessive fluid accumulation. Severe hypertension should be controlled before beginning treatment, and any cardiac conditions should be evaluated and monitored closely.

Q: How long does the benefit of the treatment last?

A: Studies suggest that relapse rates in the year following ECT are high—in the 30 to 60 percent range—unless the person is put on antidepressants or lithium.

LIGHT THERAPY

Q: What is light therapy?

A: It's usually exposure to ordinary white fluorescent light, at an intensity of 10,000 lux. That's equivalent to the amount of light exposure someone would receive from looking out a window on a sunny spring day. Typically the light is administered through a light box placed either horizontally on a desk or table or vertically on the floor.

Q: And that's used to treat depression?

A: It's used specifically to treat cases of seasonal affective disorder, or SAD.

Q: Is it effective?

A: People with SAD should respond within three to four weeks. If that's insufficient to improve the symptoms, some individuals may need to add a bright bedside lamp, on a timer, that goes on two hours before they arise. Researchers have found that a "simulated dawn" helps combat symptoms even when people are asleep during treatment.

Q: Are there side effects?

A: People have been known to develop headaches, eye-strain, irritability and insomnia, particularly if treatment is administered late at night. If that happens, they're advised to shift light therapy to the morning. Too much light exposure can induce a hypomanic or even manic episode, but this is rare and, like the other side effects, can generally be prevented by reducing exposure.

Q: Is there any other treatment for SAD?

A: People with SAD have been successfully treated with SSRIs and, to a lesser degree, with beta blockers that block the secretion of melatonin. Norman Rosenthal, an expert on SAD at NIMH, says that medication in combination with light therapy frequently produces better results than either treatment alone.

ALTERNATIVE TREATMENTS

Q: **Isn't exercise supposed to help a person feel better?**

A: Absolutely, and many therapists prescribe exercise as a partial antidote for depression. A study of clinically depressed women found that exercise, running and weight lifting all improved self-concept.

In addition to the obvious psychological benefits—exercise improves the body image and self-confidence—there are physiological, or biochemical, effects that may account for the sensation often described as "runner's high."

Q: **What are the biochemical effects?**

A: Studies show that strenuous exercise produces an increase in the body's levels of **endorphins**, compounds that affect the parts of the brain that process information about pain, emotion and feelings. It's been discovered that people who are depressed have low levels of endorphins. So increasing the level of endorphins can help mitigate or prevent someone's feelings of depression.

Q: How much exercise is needed to get that effect?

A: A person should be aerobically active—that is, his heart rate should get up to 60 to 80 percent of its maximum potential—at least three times a week, for a minimum of 20 minutes per session. But remember, check with your medical practitioner before beginning an aerobic-exercise program.

Q: Since sleep patterns seem to be a symptom of depression, can someone alleviate depression by changing the hours he sleeps?

A: It's believed in some psychotherapeutic circles that sleep deprivation—the practice of limiting sleep time—can help patients respond faster to antidepressant therapy. As a result, some psychiatrists recommend that patients sleep no more than four hours a night, preferably early in the night, for two or three nights a week. Some psychiatric hospitals in Europe keep certain depressed patients awake for an entire night a week. Sleep deprivation has also been tried in treating rapidly cycling bipolar disease.

However, sleep deprivation has been known to induce mania in some people. For that reason, it should be tried only under the supervision of a physician who's experienced in this kind of treatment.

Q: What about changes in diet or vitamin supplements?

A: Unless you're actually malnourished and have a vitamin deficit, no change in diet or vitamin, mineral or nutritional supplement is likely to affect your depressive disorder in any meaningful way, according to a consensus of psychiatrists who are experts on depression.

PROS AND CONS

Q: Which is more effective, therapy or drugs?

A: That all depends on who's answering the question. Certain mental-health professionals, including many psychiatrists, have become leading advocates of medication. Psychologists and social workers, who can't prescribe, advocate psychotherapy.

The line is somewhat fuzzier than that—many psychologists refer people to physicians for prescriptions, many psychiatrists offer insight-oriented psychotherapy. But, in general, the camp is divided along the lines mentioned above.

Q: Aren't there any studies comparing medication with psychotherapy?

A: There are numerous studies. However, their findings are often contradictory and open to conflicting interpretations.

In 1986, for example, a six-year, NIH-sponsored study came to the conclusion that cognitive therapy and interpersonal therapy were as effective as imipramine (a tricyclic) in treating people with moderate or severe depression. The study, which involved 240 people, found that at the end of 16 weeks all three treatments had eliminated serious depressive symptoms in more than half the patients.

It was a ground-breaking study because it compared two psychotherapies not only with each other but with an antidepressant, but its interpretation has proved controversial. According to Donald F. Klein, a psychiatrist who is an authority on depression, the outcome really depended on the severity of the depression.

Klein maintains that in mildly depressed patients all four treatments, including the placebo, were equally effective. But

in severely depressed patients, Klein and his co-author Paul
H. Wender, M.D., wrote in *Understanding Depression,*
"medicine was better than both psychotherapies in terms of
quickness, cost and, most important, degree of benefit."

Q: **Have there been any studies since then that have proved that medication works better than psychotherapy, or vice versa?**

A: The Depression Guideline Panel examined a total of eight studies that compared time-limited therapies (cognitive, interpersonal and behavioral) with medication, and concluded that both therapies were equally effective in treating depression in its acute phase. It noted, however, that the studies involved primarily outpatients who were not severely depressed.

In addition, the panel seemed to back medication as the best treatment for depression in the continuation phase, once the symptoms had been reduced, and as maintenance treatment, to prevent recurrences.

Q: **Aren't there any studies that find psychotherapy is more likely to prevent a recurrence?**

A: Yes, some studies have shown that certain time-limited psychotherapies have a more enduring effect than antidepressants—that is, they continue to help prevent depression long after the treatment itself has ended.

For example, a four-month trial comparing interpersonal therapy (IPT), amitriptyline (a tricyclic) and other treatments found that, one year later, there was no difference in symptoms. Furthermore, researchers rated people who had IPT as functioning better socially and as parents and family members than people who had other therapies.

Other studies find that cognitive therapy is more effective long-term than antidepressants. Martin Seligman, advocate of the learned-helplessness theory, says that his studies show that people treated with drugs tended to relapse at a far higher rate than people who got cognitive therapy.

Q: Why would psychotherapy have a more enduring effect?

A: According to Seligman, it's because drugs don't change the patient's underlying approach to life, but psychotherapy does. With cognitive therapy, he writes in *Learned Optimism,* "patients acquire a skill they can use again and again without relying on drugs or doctors. . . . Drugs seem to be activators; they push the patient up and out, but they do not make the world look any brighter. Cognitive therapy changes the way you look at things, and this new, optimistic style gets you up and around."

Q: Why are there so many totally contradictory findings?

A: One problem might be that, at least in some cases, researchers are comparing apples with oranges. For example, the University of Pittsburgh study of recurrent depression we mentioned earlier concluded that continuing medication at the same dose levels used to treat actual epi- sodes was extremely effective in preventing another episode.

In contrast, they said, regular monthly psychotherapy might help forestall a recurrence but didn't prevent it. Whether it's fair to compare acute-treatment levels with monthly psycho- therapy sessions, however, is highly debatable.

Q: So how can someone decide which treatment to follow, psychotherapy or medication?

A: Ultimately, the decision is up to the depressed person and his therapist or physician. But the Depression Guideline Panel has made a list of some factors to consider in making a decision.

According to the panel, time-limited psychotherapy may be a first-line treatment—that is, the treatment to try first—to relieve the symptoms of major depressive disorder if:

• the depression is mild to moderate, nonpsychotic, not chronic and not highly recurrent; and

• the patient desires psychotherapy as a first-line therapy.

The panel said that medication should be used first if:

• the depression is more severe
• there have been at least two prior episodes
• there's a family history of depression; and
• the patient prefers medication.

Note that the panel talks about relieving symptoms, not about eliminating the depression or preventing a recurrence —areas where it was dubious about the power of psychotherapy. That's why, when the guidelines came out, the American Psychological Association issued a press release dissociating itself, on the grounds that the guidelines "do not encourage sufficient collaboration with mental-health specialists and appear to be biased toward medication."

Q: So a patient has to choose between psychotherapy and drug treatment?

A: No, not at all. The panel, like many mental-health experts, also endorsed the combination of psychotherapy and medication. It said that, while combination therapy should not be tried routinely as the initial treatment, it was a consideration in cases where there was:

• recurrent major depressive episodes with poor interepisode recovery

• incomplete therapeutic response to either medication or psychotherapy

• patient preference; and

• evidence of a significant personality disorder. Such evidence could include the first two factors, compliance problems, troubled interpersonal relationships, multiple suicide attempts or chronic, medically unexplained physical symptoms.

Q: What are compliance problems?

A: That's when people, although still depressed, decide on their own to discontinue treatment or to curtail their treatment so much that it's ineffective. This can occur whether the treatment is medication or psychotherapy. According to one study, for example, 10 to 40 percent of psychotherapy patients fail to follow through with their full treatments. The American Psychological Association says the rate of noncompliance for people taking medication is about 60 to 70 percent.

Q: Why do people stop taking their medications or going to therapy?

A: Depressed people, almost by definition, are easily discouraged, and unless they see results immediately they may give up. The adverse side effects of antidepressants like the tricyclics may well be an additional factor. For example, in a six-week study of drug efficacy with some 500 people, 23 percent of people treated with paroxetin (an SSRI) and 36 percent of people in the group treated with imipramine (a tricyclic) withdrew because of adverse side effects.

Q: Judging from a manic-depressive poet you quoted in Chapter 5, I'd guess that people with manic depression have mixed feelings about lithium. Do they stop taking it, too?

A: Compliance is a particularly serious issue for people with manic depression who must take lithium. In their manic stages, people are easily distracted and may forget scheduled doses; they may also enjoy the manic stage and decide not to take something that brings them down to reality.

In a recent study of noncompliance by people with manic symptoms, researchers cited the main causes as intolerable side effects, prescription problems, "lack of insight"—the psychological term for a failure to establish links between the present and one's past—and, related to that, the belief that they no longer need medication.

Q: And psychotherapy can improve compliance?

A: Yes. It can help a depressed person come to terms with taking the drug and with the changes—positive and negative, such as side effects—that the drug may make in her life.

In his book, *Listening to Prozac,* Peter Kramer describes one patient who makes a poor adjustment to Prozac. The reason, the psychiatrist writes, is that the patient hadn't been prepared through psychotherapy to deal with the generally positive personality changes that resulted from his taking the drug. Kramer, an unabashed advocate of Prozac, says, "We'd be very mistaken to jettison psychotherapy or Freud."

Q: You've been discussing the various treatments for major depression. What's best for dysthymia: psychotherapy or medication?

A: For years, because it was understood as a personality disorder rather than as a form of depression, dysthymia was treated mostly through psychotherapy. However, there's growing evidence that antidepressants, including TCAs and MAOIs, are effective against dysthymia.

For example, a 1988 study by James Kocsis, a dysthymia expert at Cornell Medical Center, New York, published in the *Archives of General Psychiatry,* reported that 6 out of 10 people with dysthymia responded to antidepressants. But dysthymia is a stubborn condition. Kocsis also found that, even among dysthymics who hadn't had any symptoms for at least six months, there was a relapse rate of 55 to 60 percent after they discontinued medication.

Q: How does that compare with results from psychotherapy?

A: Psychologists tend to maintain that, in the long run, psychotherapy is more effective, partly because it teaches dysthymics the coping mechanisms they need. James McCullough of Virginia Commonwealth University says that a combination of cognitive and behavior therapy was still effective for about two-thirds of his patients two years later.

7 DEPRESSION AND THE WORKPLACE

Q: If I'm depressed, do I have to tell my employer?

A: You're not required to tell anyone, including your employer, if you're suffering from a mood disorder. However, if your condition is affecting your performance, it could be to your benefit to tell your employer why.

The 1990 Americans With Disabilities Act (ADA) provides a number of protections that can help you, but only if you put yourself in a position to take advantage of them. If you're having difficulty coping with the demands of your job, you can claim protection under ADA—but obviously, you'll have to forgo some confidentiality about your condition.

Q: Does ADA cover anyone who's suffering from depression or other mood disorders?

A: It's not that sweeping. For one thing, ADA covers only workplaces with at least 15 employees. For another, it covers people whose disabilities are deemed to substantially limit one or more major life activities. Such activities include caring for oneself, performing manual tasks, walking and working.

In general, it's fairly safe to say that major depressive disorder and manic depression meet ADA criteria. In the past, some employers have tried to argue that manic depression is emotional, not mental, and therefore not covered, but they've generally lost their cases in court. ADA regulations specifically allow mental impairments that include emotional disorders. However, a less-debilitating mood disorder like dysthymia might not meet ADA criteria.

Q: What protection, specifically, does ADA provide? Does it mean I can't be fired?

A: No, it provides no absolute protection against firing. The extent to which you're protected depends on the nature of your depression and of your job, and also on your employer's policy regarding people with physical disabilities.

As a rule, to keep your job you must be able to perform its essential functions, and you cannot act in ways that disrupt the workplace. You do have a right to ask your employer for what the law calls "reasonable accommodation." And your employer is expected to make approximately comparable accommodation for physically and mentally disabled employees.

Q: What's reasonable accommodation?

A: It's assistance that enables you to perform your job. This ranges from flexible scheduling, to allow you to visit a therapist or clinic, to restructuring your job duties to providing extra unpaid leave for short-term psychiatric treatment.

For example, if you have weekly therapy appointments, your employer might allow you to take a two-hour or longer lunch period once a week and make up the work at another time. But you're not entitled to a reduction in the total number of hours you work.

Q: Can an employer refuse reasonable accommodation?

A: Precisely what's reasonable is open to interpretation. If you had an office job and said you needed a quiet place to work, for example, your employer would probably be compelled to provide it. If, on the other hand, you worked in a factory, your employer might say that your request is unreasonable, and the court might support him.

Q: What does ADA say about treatment?

A: You cannot be fired, as people have in the past, for being in psychotherapy or for taking psychopharmaceuticals. In fact, you can be fired if you refuse to take medication or participate in treatment and you're thus unable to do your job.

You're still covered by ADA if you're taking medication that alleviates your symptoms, such as lithium for manic depression. And if the medication is causing certain side effects, then your employer must provide reasonable accommodation for them—for example, letting you make notes or use a tape recorder if you're having memory problems.

Q: What if I'm looking for work? Do I have to tell prospective employers?

A: No. In fact, that's probably the area where the law gives you the most protection. You don't have to volunteer any information about past or present psychiatric problems, and prospective employees may not ask you about such problems. If they do learn that you have a history of depression, they cannot refuse to hire you because they think you might be unable to perform essential job functions sometime in the future, or because they're afraid that job stress might trigger a relapse.

Once you're hired, you cannot be fired if your employer discovers you've been previously hospitalized for depression. And you can't be denied a promotion because your employer thinks you'd crack under the stress.

Q: **Even with the ADA protection, aren't I better off concealing the fact that I am or have been depressed?**

A: That depends on your employer. Unfortunately, many companies are still not enlightened about mental illness, and may challenge in court your claim to protection under ADA. In such cases, secrecy may well be the best course.

However, by concealing your depression, you're less likely to get the help you need. While you're not required to tell your employer that you're depressed (and possibly you shouldn't), be sure you share your problem with someone— a friend, family member or professional helper. Remember, with time and help, most depressed people do recover.

INFORMATIONAL AND MUTUAL-AID GROUPS

American Association of Retired Persons (AARP)
Widowed Persons Services
Social Outreach and Support
1909 K St. N.W.
Washington, DC 20049
202-728-4370

Depression After Delivery
P.O. Box 1282
Morrisville, PA 19067
215-295-3994

**Depression Awareness, Recognition, and Treatment
  (D/ART)**
National Institute of Mental Health
5600 Fishers Ln., Room 10-85
Rockville, MD 20857
301-443-4140

Lithium Information Center
8000 Excelsior Dr., Suite 302
Madison, WI 53717
608-836-8070

National Alliance for the Mentally Ill (NAMI)
NAMI CAN (Children and Adolescents Network)
SAC (Siblings and Adult Children's) Network
2101 Wilson Blvd., Suite 302
Arlington, VA 22201
800-950-NAMI

National Depressive and Manic Depressive Association
53 W. Jackson Blvd., Suite 618
Chicago, IL 60604
800-82N-DMDA

National Foundation for Depressive Illness
P.O. Box 2257
New York, NY 10116
800-248-4344

National Mental Health Association
1021 Prince St.
Alexandria, VA 22314
800-969-NMHA

National Organization for Seasonal Affective Disorder
   (NOSAD)
P.O. Box 40133
Washington, DC 20016

Society for Light Treatment and Biological Rhythms
P.O. Box 478
Wilsonville, OR 97070

GLOSSARY

Acute treatment: Formally defined procedures, either pharmacological or psychotherapeutic, used to reduce and remove the sights and symptoms of depression and to restore psychosocial functions.

Adjustment disorder: A normal and temporary reaction of grief to stress, such as the loss of a loved one.

Affective disorder: A disorder in which one's affect, or mood, is subject to change to extreme sadness or excitement or both. The term is used to describe both depression and mania.

Agoraphobia: A form of phobia characterized by a fear of open, public places or of crowds.

Anhedonia: The inability to experience pleasure from any activity.

Anorexia nervosa: An eating disorder in which the individual, intensely fearful of becoming fat, refuses to maintain body weight over a minimal normal weight.

Anticholinergic: The tendency of some antidepressants, by counteracting the activity of the neurotransmitter acetylcholine, to produce certain side effects, including dry mouth, blurred vision, constipation and difficulty in urination.

Antidepressants: Drugs used to treat depression.

Anxiety disorder: A psychological disorder in which the individual suffers from inappropriate and excessive degrees of physical and mental symptoms of anxiety, such as apprehension, restlessness, fast heartbeat and respiration.

Atypical depression: A form of depression characterized by oversleeping and overeating, little energy and an extreme sensitivity to rejection, particularly romantic rejection.

Behavioral therapy: A psychotherapeutic approach that seeks to change behavior and teach coping techniques rather than alter the underlying personality.

Bipolar disorder: See **Manic-depressive disorder.**

Bulimia: A chronic eating disorder characterized by recurrent episodes of binge eating and self-induced vomiting and a feeling of lack of control.

Clinical depression: Any depression where symptoms are severe and lasting enough to require treatment.

Clinical social worker: A mental-health professional, typically with a master's degree in social work, who is trained to offer psychotherapy.

Cognitive therapy: A psychotherapeutic approach based on the concepts that depression is the result of unduly pessimistic ways of thinking and distorted attitudes about oneself, the world and the future. It seeks to correct these notions.

Continuation treatment: Treatment designed to prevent the return of the most recent episode of a mood disorder.

Cortisol: A steroid hormone that is secreted during prolonged stress of any kind.

Cyclothymia: A form of manic depression, lasting at least two years, characterized by short mood swings between low mood, inactivity and fatigue and high mood, high energy and overconfidence.

Dementia: A group of mental disorders involving a general loss of intellectual abilities, including memory, judgment and abstract thinking.

Depression: Persistent feelings of sadness, despair and discouragement, which may be a symptom of an underlying mental or physical disorder or a specific mental disorder.

Dexamethasone: A synthetic steroid that normally suppresses the production of cortisol.

Diuretic: Something that tends to increase the discharge of urine.

Dopamine: A neurotransmitter in the brain thought to be associated with depression.

Double depression: The combination of dysthymia plus major depression.

Dysthymia: A chronic, mild depression that is present most of the time for at least two years.

Electroconvulsive therapy (ECT) (or Electroshock therapy): A form of therapy, usually reserved for very severe or psychotic depressions or manic states, in which low-voltage electric current is sent to the brain to induce a convulsion or seizure.

Electroencephalogram (EEG): A record of brain patterns, collected by placing electrodes on the scalp, that is often used to detect brain damage.

Endorphins: Compounds that affect the parts of the brain that process information about pain, emotion and feelings. Low levels of endorphins have been related to depression.

Family systems: A psychotherapeutic orientation that examines the family's historic pattern of interaction.

Family therapist: A mental-health practitioner offering counseling services. See Family therapy.

Family therapy (or marital/couples and family therapy):
Psychotherapeutic treatment of marital partners or
parents and children.

Feminist psychotherapy: A form of psychotherapy that
views depression as a natural reaction to the oppression of women in society, and tries to eliminate the
depression through empowerment.

Hypersomnia: Sleep of excessive frequency or duration.

Hypomania: A form of manic depression in which severe
depressions alternate with mild elevations of mood
and activity.

Hypothyroidism: Reduced thyroid function; a condition
whose symptoms may mimic those of depression.

Insight-oriented: A psychotherapeutic approach in which
the therapist tries to help patients gain an insight
into the roots of their problems or an increased
awareness of their unconscious motivations.

Interpersonal psychotherapy (IPT): A time-limited form
of psychodynamic psychotherapy that focuses on
current interpersonal relationships and teaches more
effective ways of relating to others and coping with
conflicts in relationships.

Light therapy: A form of therapy in which the individual is
exposed to bright artificial light of exceptionally
high intensity.

Lithium: A natural salt that is the primary treatment for
manic-depressive disorder.

Magnetic resonance imaging (MRI): An imaging technique
that produces detailed pictures of the brain or other
areas inside the body, by linking a computer with a
powerful magnet.

Maintenance treatment: Treatment designed to prevent a
new mood episode.

Major depressive disorder: A clinical depression that meets specific diagnostic criteria as to duration, functional impairment and involvement of a cluster of both physiological and psychological symptoms.

Manic-depressive disorder (or bipolar disorder): A disorder in which bouts of major depression alternate with mania, a condition characterized by energetic, risk-taking, impulsive and often self-destructive behavior.

MAOIs: See **Monoamine oxidase inhibitors.**

Melancholic depression: A severe form of major depression marked by a failure to take interest or pleasure in all, or almost all, activities, or to make even brief, temporary mood improvements.

Monoamine oxidase inhibitors (MAOIs): A group of antidepressant drugs that inhibit the action of monoamine oxidase, thus increasing the concentration of monoamines at the synapse.

Mood disorder: A category of psychiatric conditions that have, as a central feature, a disturbance in mood—usually profound sadness or apathy, euphoria or irritability.

Neurotransmitter: A chemical substance that transmits nerve impulses across synaptic junctions, or the microscopic gaps between nerve endings.

Norepinephrine: A neurotransmitter found in the brain, low levels of which have been linked to depression.

Obsessive-compulsive disorder: A form of anxiety disorder involving repetitive thoughts and behaviors—such as constant handwashing or checking—that are difficult, if not impossible, to control.

Panic disorder: A form of anxiety disorder characterized by discrete intense periods of fear, for no obvious cause, and other symptoms.

Personality disorder: A psychiatric illness, not uncommon among people with mood disorder, characterized by behavior and beliefs that are excessively odd, emotional, erratic, anxious or fearful.

Pharmacotherapy: In conjunction with psychotherapy, the use of pharmacological agents in the treatment of mental disorders.

Phobic disorder: A form of anxiety disorder characterized by persistent and irrational fears, usually of specific objects, activities or situations.

Phototherapy: See **Light therapy.**

Postpartum depression (PPD): A severe and long-lasting depression that, for some women, follows childbirth.

Premenstrual dysphoric disorder (PMDD): A pattern of severe, recurrent symptoms of depression and other negative mood states that typically occurs in the last week of the menstrual cycle and can disappear once menstruation begins.

Pseudodementia: A form of depression in which memory seems to fade, and complicated thinking and concentration become difficult.

Psychiatric nurse specialist: A registered nurse (R.N.), usually with a master's degree in psychiatric nursing, who specializes in treating mental or psychiatric disorders.

Psychiatrist: A physician who specializes in the diagnosis and treatment of mental or psychiatric disorders.

Psychoanalysis: The most open-ended and undirected of the psychotherapeutic approaches, in which patients may spend years seeking insights into the roots of their problems or an increased awareness of their unconscious motivations.

Psychodynamic therapy: A psychotherapeutic approach that focuses on the underlying drives and desires that determine behavior.

Psychoeducation: Educating the patient's family to help stabilize his or her home environment and help him or her react constructively to the illness and treatment.

Psychologist: A person with a doctoral degree (Ph.D. or Psy.D.) in psychology and training in counseling, psychotherapy and psychological testing.

Psychomotor agitation: Excessively rapid or frenetic motor actions directly proceeding from mental activity.

Psychomotor retardation: Excessively slow or sluggish motor actions directly proceeding from mental activity.

Psychopharmacology: The study of the effects of psycho-active drugs on behavior in both animals and people. Clinical psychopharmacology more specifically includes both the study of drug effects in patients and the expert use of drugs in the treatment of psychiatric conditions.

Psychosis: A mental illness characterized by defective or lost contact with reality, often with hallucinations or delusions.

Psychosocial: Description of psychological and/or social factors that may play a role in precipitating depression.

Psychosomatic: A term describing the mind-body relationship. It is used to describe disorders in which psychological factors play a crucial role in leading to physical disease.

Psychotherapy: Therapy employing psychological methods ranging from psychoanalysis to behavioral modification.

Psychotic depression: Depression with psychotic features, such as delusions or hallucinations.

Rational-emotive therapy (RET): A form of cognitive therapy, developed by psychologist Albert Ellis, that presupposes people create their own emotional problems through illogical thinking or irrational beliefs.

Retrograde amnesia: Failure to recall events within a few months before and after a treatment with electroconvulsive therapy.

Reuptake: The absorption of a neurotransmitter by the presynaptic neuron—the cell from which the neurotransmitter is released—before it can pass to another cell.

Seasonal affective disorder (SAD): A depressive condition apparently triggered by the onset of winter and the diminution of hours of sunlight.

Selective serotonin reuptake inhibitor (SSRI): An antidepressant agent that primarily inhibits the reuptake of serotonin.

Serotonin: A neurotransmitter found in the brain, low levels of which have been linked to depression.

Supportive therapy: Short-term therapy that emphasizes supporting, rather than changing, the person who is depressed.

Synapse: The microscopic gap between nerve endings where one cell meets another.

Syndrome: A constellation of signs and symptoms indicative of an illness or disorder.

Tricyclic antidepressant (TCA): A type of antidepressant, named for its three-ring chemical structure, widely prescribed for people with major depressive disorder.

Unipolar depression: Major depression that, unlike bipolar depression, does not alternate with mania.

Vegetative: Descriptive of a type of behavior that includes oversleeping and overeating.

SUGGESTED READING

Beck, Aaron T. *Love Is Never Enough.* New York: Harper & Row, 1988.

Braiker, Harriet B. *Getting Up When You're Feeling Down: A Woman's Guide to Overcoming and Preventing Depression.* New York: G.P. Putnam's Sons, 1988.

Breggin, Peter R. *Toxic Psychiatry.* New York: St. Martin's Press, 1991.

Burns, David D. *The Feeling Good Handbook.* New York: William Morrow, 1989.

Chan, Connie S. *If It Runs in Your Family: Depression.* New York: Bantam Books, 1993.

Coyne, James C., ed. *Essential Papers on Depression.* New York: New York University Press, 1985.

Cronkite, Kathy. *On the Edge of Darkness: Conversations About Conquering Depression.* New York: Doubleday, 1994.

DePaulo, J. Raymond, Jr., and Keith Russell Ablow. *How to Cope With Depression: A Complete Guide for You and Your Family.* New York: McGraw-Hill, 1989.

Dowling, Colette. *You Mean I Don't **Have** to Feel This Way?* New York: Scribner's, 1991.

Duke, Patty, and Gloria Hochman. *A Brilliant Madness: Living With Manic-Depressive Illness.* New York: Bantam Books, 1992.

Ellis, Albert. *How to Stubbornly Refuse to Make Yourself Miserable About Anything—Yes, Anything!* Secaucus, N.J.: Lyle Stuart, 1988.

Engler, Jack, and Daniel Goleman. *The Consumer's Guide to Psychotherapy*. New York: Simon & Schuster/Fireside, 1992.

Fieve, Ronald R. *Moodswing*. New York: Bantam Books, 1989.

———. *Prozac: Questions & Answers for Patients, Family and Physicians*. New York: Avon, 1994.

Goldberg, Ivan K. *Questions & Answers About Depression and Its Treatment*. Philadelphia: The Charles Press, 1993.

Gorman, Jack. *The Essential Guide to Psychiatric Drugs*. New York: St. Martin's Press, 1990.

Hirschfeld, Robert. *When the Blues Won't Go Away*. New York: Macmillan, 1991.

Jamison, Kay Redfield. *Touched With Fire: Manic-Depressive Illness and the Artistic Temperament*. New York: The Free Press/Macmillan, 1993.

Klein, Donald F., and Paul H. Wender. *Understanding Depression*. New York: Oxford University Press, 1993.

Kline, Nathan S. *From Sad to Glad*. New York: G.P. Putnam's Sons, 1974.

Kramer, Peter D. *Listening to Prozac*. New York: Viking, 1993.

McGrath, Ellen. *When Feeling Bad Is Good*. New York: Henry Holt and Company, 1992.

McGrath, Ellen, et al, ed. *Women and Depression*. Washington, D.C.: American Psychological Association, 1990.

Millett, Kate. *The Loony Bin Trip*. New York: Simon and Schuster, 1990.

Mondimore, Francis M. *Depression: The Mood Disease*. Baltimore, Md.: Johns Hopkins University Press, 1990.

Papolos, Demitri F., and Janice Papolos. *Overcoming Depression*. New York: Harper & Row, 1987.

Rosenthal, Norman E. *Winter Blues*. New York: Guilford Press, 1993.

Seligman, Martin E.P. *Learned Optimism*. New York: Alfred A. Knopf, 1990.

Shapiro, Patricia Gottlieb. *A Parent's Guide to Childhood and Adolescent Depression (The Children's Hospital of Philadelphia Series)*. New York: Dell Publishing, 1994.

Styron, William. *Darkness Visible: A Memoir of Madness*. New York: Random House, 1990.

INDEX

A

AA. *See* Alcoholics Anonymous (AA)

Abdominal pain, depression diagnosis and, 17

Abuse, physical/sexual, effects of, 56, 63-64, 71

Acquired immunodeficiency virus. *See* AIDS

Acute treatment, defined, 169

ADA. *See* The 1990 Americans With Disabilities Act (ADA)

Adjustment disorders
  defined, 11, 169
  versus depression, 11

Adolescence
  dysthymia and, 25
  manic-depressive disorder and, 25
  symptoms of depression in, 34

Advil. *See* Ibuprofen

Affective disorder
  defined, 11, 169
  suicide in adolescents with, 40

Age, effects of, 29, 31-34

Agoraphobia
  defined, 169
  effects of, 39

AIDS, effects of, 47

Alcohol abuse
  effects of, 31, 36-38, 56
  manic-depressive disorder and, 22

Alcoholics Anonymous (AA), antidepressants and, 120

Alternative treatments
  diet, 154
  exercise, 153-154
  sleep deprivation, 154
  vitamin supplements, 154

Alzheimer's disease
  depression treatment and, 77
  effects of, 69
  misdiagnosis of, 32

The 1990 Americans With Disabilities Act (ADA), 163-166

Amish culture, 31

Amitriptyline. *See* Tricyclic antidepressants (TCAs)

Amphetamines, effects of, 49

Anger, psychoanalysis and, 49-50

Anhedonia, defined, 18, 169

Anorexia nervosa
  defined, 169
  effects of, 38

Anti-inflammatory agents, lithium and, 141

Antibiotics, lithium and, 141

179

Anticholinergic side effects, defined, 127, 169

Anticonvulsants, lithium alternatives, 138, 142-143

Antidepressants. *See also* Prozac
Alzheimer's disease and, 77
for children, 124-125
combination of, 122-23
comparison of, 120-21
compliance problems with, 159, 161
computer-assisted therapy and, 117
contraindications, 124
controversy about, 119-20
defined, 119, 169
discontinuation, 123
for elderly, 125
lithium combined with, 138
long-term use of, 81
primary-care doctors and, 83
psychiatrists and, 85
recurrence, 124
thyroid supplements and, 122
types of, 120, 135

Anxiety disorder
defined, 170
depression, 38

Apathy, depression diagnosis and, 12

Aplastic anemia, carbamazepine and, 143

Appetite, depression diagnosis and, 12

Arthritis
antidepressants and, 124
lithium and, 124

Aspirin, lithium and, 141

Assertiveness training, behavioral therapy and, 98-99

Attribution style, 58-59

Atypical depression
defined, 19, 170
treatment, 129

B

Backaches, depression diagnosis and, 17

BDI. *See* Beck Depression Inventory (BDI)

Beck Depression Inventory (BDI), 14

Behavioral therapy
defined, 96, 170
recurrence with, 156
tasks/tactics in, 97-100

Benzodiazepine, side effects, 49

Bereavement, effects of, 50-52, 54

Beta blockers
antidepressants and, 124
combined with light therapy, 152

Biological treatments. *See* Electro-convulsive therapy (ECT); Light therapy

Bipolar disorder. *See also* Manic-depressive disorder
defined, 15, 21, 170, 173
famous artists and writers with, 22

Blood pressure, antidepressants and, 124

Bowel disorders, effects of, 17

Breast cancer, antidepressants and, 124

Bulimia
buproprion and, 136-137
defined, 170
effects of, 38

Buproprion
mechanism of action, 136
side effects, 136-137

C

Cabin fever, seasonal affective disorder (SAD) and, 24

Cancer
breast, antidepressants and, 124
depression treatment with, 77
effects of, 36-37, 47, 49

mood disorder and, 47
suicide and, 47
Carbamazepine
  as lithium alternative, 142-143
  side effects, 143
Carbohydrates, seasonal affective
  disorder (SAD) and, 73
Causes
  biochemical factors, 41-49
  biological, 41-49
  psychosocial, 41, 49-59
Cavett, Dick, electroconvulsive
  therapy (ECT) and, 147
Center for Epidemiological Studies
  —Depression Scale (CES-D), 14
CES-D. *See* Center for
  Epidemiological Studies—
  Depression Scale (CES-D)
Childbirth. *See also* Postpartum
  depression (PPD)
  effects of, 60
Children
  antidepressants and, 124-125
  Children's Depression Inventory,
    14
  depression
    causes, 71
    diagnosis, 14
    incidence, 33
    symptoms, 33-34
  depression in women with, 64-65
  dysthymia in, 25, 34
  psychotherapy efficacy, 114
  suicide rate for, 39-40
Children's Depression Inventory, 14
Chlorpromazine, lithium combined
  with, 138
Chronic fatigue syndrome, versus
  depression, 47
Churchill, Winston, depression
  and, 27
Cibalith. *See* Lithium
Clinical depression, defined, 11, 170
Clinical social worker, defined,
  84, 170

Cocaine, effects of, 49
Cognitive/behavioral therapy
  in children, 114
  defined, 89
  effects of, 112-114, 161
Cognitive therapy
  Beck, Aaron T., 100-103
  defined, 96, 100-101, 170
  Rational-Emotive Therapy (RET),
    104-105
  recurrence with, 156-157
Compliance
  psychotherapy versus medication
    and, 159-160
  support groups for lithium, 112
Computer-assisted therapy
  defined, 116
  efficacy, 116-117
Contact lenses, tricyclic antidepressants (TCAs) and, 128
Continuation treatment, defined,
  80, 170
Contraceptives, oral, side effects,
  49, 60
Conversation skills, behavioral
  therapy and, 98-99
Cortisol
  defined, 43, 170
  depression and, 43-44
  hypothalamic-pituitary-adrenal
    (HPA) axis and, 43
  postpartum depression (PPD)
    and, 61
Costs in United States, depression,
  12
Cyclothymia, defined, 24, 170

D

Death. *See also* Stress Scale
  parental, effects of, 50-51, 56, 71
Dementia, defined, 15, 171
Depakote. *See* Valproate
Depression
  versus adjustment disorders, 11

after head injury, 47
age at onset, 29
atypical
   defined, 19, 170
   treatment, 129
      monoamine oxidase
         inhibitors (MAOIs), 129
biochemical factors, 41-49
biological causes, 41-49
bipolar, defined, 15, 21, 170, 173
cancer and, 36-37, 47, 49
clinical, defined, 11, 170
cortisol and, 43-44
costs in United States, 12
defined, 11, 171
diagnosis
   criteria for, 12-13
   dexamethasone suppression
      test (DST), 43-44
double, defined, 20-21, 171
endocrine disorders and, 42-44
etiology, 28
forms of, 18-25
Freudian view of, 49-50
history, 26-27
hypothalamic-pituitary-adrenal
   (HPA) axis and, 43
hypothyroidism and, 15, 43, 47
incidence
   in females, 25
   generally, 25-30
   in males, 25
manic. See Manic-depressive
   disorder
medications and, 49
melancholic, defined, 18, 173
men and, 31
misdiagnosis of, 76
mistreatment of, 76-77
neurotic. See Dysthymia
neurotransmitters and, 41-42
nontreatment of, 29
physical illness and, generally,
   35-40

postpartum (PPD), defined,
   61, 174
predisposition to, 56-57
psychosocial causes, 41, 49-59
psychotic, defined, 18, 175
residual symptoms, 79-80
risk factors for recurrence, 29-30
signs/symptoms, 12-13
treatment. See also specific types
   of depression
   costs of, 85, 87
   criteria for seeking, 82
   medical insurance for, 87, 116
   overview, 75-87
   private versus clinic, 86-87
   professionals for, 83-85
unipolar, defined, 15, 176
Depression episode, length of, 29
Depression Guideline Panel
   medication versus psychotherapy
      and, 78, 128, 133, 156-159
   U.S. Department of Health and
      Human Services, 16
Depressive personality disorder,
   defined, 56
Desipramine. See Tricyclic antidepressants (TCAs)
Desyrel. See Trazodone
Dexamethasone, defined, 43, 171
Dexamethasone suppression test
   (DST), depression diagnosis
   with, 43-44
Diabetes, effects of, 36, 47-48, 78
Diagnosis, criteria for, 12-13
Diagnostic and Statistical Manual
   of Mental Disorders (DSM-IV),
   criteria for diagnosis of
   depression, 12-13
Diet
   effects of, 154
   lithium and, 141
   monoamine oxidase inhibitors
      (MAOIs) and, 130-131, 141
Digitalis, side effects, 49
Diuretics, lithium and, 141

Divorce. *See also* Stress Scale
effects of, 56, 71
Dopamine
buproprion and, 136
defined, 42, 171
mood disorders and, 42
Double depression, defined, 20-21, 171
Drug abuse
effects of, 31, 38, 49
manic-depressive disorder and, 22
DST. *See* Dexamethasone suppression test (DST)
Duke, Patty, manic-depressive disorder and, 139
Dysthymia
cause, 45
children and, 34
defined, 19, 75, 171
incidence, 25
nontreatment of, 29
treatment, 129
cognitive/behavioral therapy, 161
monoamine oxidase inhibitors (MAOIs), 129, 161
psychotherapy versus medication, 161
tricyclic antidepressants (TCAs), 161

E

Eating disorders, effects of, 38
ECT. *See* Electroconvulsive therapy (ECT)
EEG. *See* Electroencephalogram (EEG)
Effexor. *See* Venlafaxine
Elavil. *See* Tricyclic antidepressants (TCAs)
Elderly
antidepressants and, 125
depression
incidence, 32-33, 70
psychosocial factors, 69-70

electroconvulsive therapy (ECT) for, 150
methylphenidate for, 137
selective serotonin reuptake inhibitors (SSRIs) and, 134
suicide rate for, 39-40
Electroconvulsive therapy (ECT)
Cavett, Dick and, 147
defined, 145, 171
elderly and, 150
history/incidence, 146-147
Horowitz, Vladimir and, 148
mechanism of action, 146
relapse after, 151
side effects, 147-148, 150
treatment qualifications, 149
Electroencephalogram (EEG)
defined, 15, 171
depression diagnosis and, 15
Electroshock therapy. *See* Electroconvulsive therapy (ECT)
Employment. *See also* Stress Scale
The 1990 Americans With Disabilities Act (ADA), 163-166
behavioral therapy and, 100
effects of, 65-69
Empowerment, feminist psychotherapy and, 106-107
Endocrine disorders
effects of, 42-44
mood disorders and, 42-44
Endorphins
defined, 153, 171
effects of, 153
Energy loss, depression diagnosis and, 13
Environmental interventions, behavioral therapy and, 100
Epilepsy drugs, manic-depressive disorder and, 138, 142-143
Epstein-Barr disease, versus depression, 47
Eskalith. *See* Lithium
Estrogen replacement therapy, selective serotonin reuptake inhibitors (SSRIs) and, 134

Exercise, effects of, 153-154
Explanatory style, 58-59

F

Family systems, defined, 108, 171
Family therapist, defined, 84, 171
Family therapy
  defined, 107, 172
  focus of, 107-109
  historical perspective, 108
  interactional perspective, 108-109
  length of, 110
  licensing in, 84-85
Fatigue, depression diagnosis and, 13, 17
Fees, mental-health practitioner, 85
Feminist psychotherapy, defined, 106-107, 172
Fluoxetine. See Prozac
Freud, Sigmund, 49-50
Freudian view of depression, 49-50

G

Gastrointestinal disorders, effects of, 17
General Health Questionnaire (GHQ), 14
Genetics
  depression and, 41, 44-45
  dysthymia and, 45
  manic-depressive disorders and, 45-46
  mood disorders and, 45
  seasonal affective disorder (SAD) and, 73
GHQ. See General Health Questionnaire (GHQ)
Group therapy
  efficacy in adolescents, 114
  versus individual, 110-111
  versus support groups, 111-112
Guilt, depression diagnosis and, 13

H

Haldol. See Haloperidol
Haloperidol, lithium combined with, 138
Head injury, depression after, 47
Headaches, recurring, depression diagnosis and, 17
Heart disease
  effects of, 36, 47-48, 77
  selective serotonin reuptake inhibitors (SSRIs) and, 134
  tricyclic antidepressants (TCAs) and, 128
Hemingway, Ernest, manic-depressive disorder and, 22
Hepatitis
  carbamazepine and, 143
  valproate, 143
History, depression, 26-27
Hormones
  mood disorders and, 42-43
  seasonal affective disorder (SAD) and, 73
  selective serotonin reuptake inhibitors (SSRIs) and, 134
Horowitz, Vladimir, electroconvulsive therapy (ECT) and, 148
Hospitalization, criteria for, 78
Hypersomnia
  defined, 172
  depression diagnosis and, 12
Hyperthyroidism, manic-depressive disorder symptoms and, 42-43
Hypomania, defined, 24, 172
Hypothalamic-pituitary-adrenal (HPA) axis, cortisol and, 43
Hypothyroidism
  defined, 15, 172
  effects of, 15, 43, 47

I

Ibuprofen, lithium and, 141
Illness, chronic, children versus adults and, 71

Imipramine. *See* Tricyclic antidepressants (TCAs)

Immune system, effects of, 35

Indigestion, depression diagnosis
and, 17

Infertility, effects of, 60

Informational and mutual-aid
groups, 167-168

Insight-oriented therapy, defined,
89, 172

Insomnia, depression diagnosis
and, 12, 17

Interpersonal psychotherapy (IPT)
criticism of, 95
defined, 93, 172
efficacy, 113
focus of, 93-95
recurrence with, 156-157

IPT. *See* Interpersonal psychotherapy (IPT)

Irritable-bowel syndrome, effects
of, 17

Isocarboxazid. *See* Monoamine
oxidase inhibitors (MAOIs)

K

Kidney dysfunction, effects of, 47

L

Learned helplessness, 57-59, 67, 70

Learning disabilities, effects of, 71

Light therapy
combined with beta blockers or
selective serotonin reuptake
inhibitors (SSRIs), 152
defined, 151, 172
seasonal affective disorder (SAD)
and, 152-153
side effects, 152

Lithane. *See* Lithium

Lithium
alternatives, 142-143
brand names, 137-138
compliance with, 112, 160

contraindications, 124, 142
defined, 120, 137, 172
dosage, 140
drug interactions with, 141
mechanism of action, 138
side effects, 139-141
support groups and, 112
toxicity, 142
treatment period, 140-141

Lithobid. *See* Lithium

Liver dysfunction, effects of, 47

Lowell, Robert, manic-depressive
disorder and, 139

M

Magnetic resonance imaging (MRI),
defined, 15, 172

Maintenance treatment
conditions for, 80-81
defined, 80, 172
recurrence and, 115

Major depressive disorder, defined,
13, 173

Mania. *See* Manic-depressive
disorder

Manic depression. *See* Manic-
depressive disorder

Manic-depressive disorder. *See also*
Bipolar disorder
after head injury, 47
cause, 45-46
defined, 21, 173
forms of, 23-24
gender and, 46
incidence, 26
mixed mood disorder with,
23, 142-143
neurotransmitters and, 41-42
symptoms, 22
treatment, 112, 120
anticonvulsants, 138, 142-143
chlorpromazine, 138
haloperidol, 138
lithium, 112, 120, 124,
137-143, 160

MAOIs. *See* Monoamine oxidase inhibitors (MAOIs)

Marriage. *See also* Family therapy; Stress Scale
  behavioral therapy and, 100
  effects of, 64-65
  family, and child counseling, licensing in, 84-85
  family therapy and, 84

Medical disorders, versus depression symptoms, 16-17, 47-48

Medical insurance, 87, 116

Medication. *See also* specific types of
  versus psychotherapy, 78, 155-161
  side effects, 49

Melancholia, 26

Melancholic depression, defined, 18, 173

Melatonin, seasonal affective disorder (SAD) and, 73

Memory
  electroconvulsive therapy (ECT) and, 147-148, 150
  recovering, 64

Men
  depression and, 31
  manic-depressive disorder and, 46

Menopause, effects of, 62-63

Menstrual cycle, effects of, 62

Mental-health professionals, generally, 82-87

Mental illness, stigma attached to, 17

Mental-status examination, 14-15

Methylphenidate, for elderly, 137

Migraines, antidepressants and, 124

Minorities
  interpersonal psychotherapy (IPT) and, 95
  mental illness and, 17

Miscarriage, effects of, 60

Mixed mood disorder, manic-depressive disorder with, 23, 142-143

Monoamine oxidase inhibitors (MAOIs)
  mechanism of action, 129
  side effects, 130, 134

Mononucleosis, versus depression, 47

Mood disorder
  cancer and, 47
  cause, 45
  defined, 11, 173
  dopamine and, 42
  endocrine disorders and, 42-44
  hormonal imbalance and, 42-43
  mental-status examination and, 15

Mother, death of, effects of, 50-51

Motrin. *See* Ibuprofen

MRI. *See* Magnetic resonance imaging (MRI)

N

Nardil. *See* Monoamine oxidase inhibitors (MAOIs)

Neurasthenia, 26

Neurotic depression. *See* Dysthymia

Neurotransmitters
  defined, 41-42, 173
  depression and, 41-42
  electroconvulsive therapy (ECT) and, 146
  manic-depressive disorder and, 41-42
  monoamine oxidase inhibitors (MAOIs) and, 129
  seasonal affective disorder (SAD) and, 73

Norepinephrine
  defined, 42, 173
  monoamine oxidase inhibitors (MAOIs) and, 129
  tricyclic antidepressants (TCAs) and, 126

Norplant, side effects, 49

Nortriptyline. *See* Tricyclic antidepressants (TCAs)

Nuprin. *See* Ibuprofen

O

Obsessive-compulsive disorders
defined, 173
effects of, 38
Oral contraceptives, side effects,
49, 60

P

Panic disorder
defined, 173
effects of, 38-39
Parkinson's disease, effects of, 47
Parnate. *See* Monoamine oxidase
inhibitors (MAOIs)
Paroxetine. *See* Selective serotonin
reuptake inhibitors (SSRIs)
Paxil. *See* Selective serotonin
reuptake inhibitors (SSRIs)
Permanence, 58
Personality disorder, defined,
20, 174
Personalization, 59
Pervasiveness, 59
Pharmacotherapy
clinical depression and, 75
defined, 174
Phenelzine. *See* Monoamine oxidase
inhibitors (MAOIs)
Phobic disorder
defined, 174
depression, 38
Phototherapy. *See* Light therapy
Physical abuse, effects of, 56,
63-64, 71
Physical illness, depression and,
generally, 35-40
Plath, Sylvia, depression treatment
and, 79
Play therapy, efficacy in children,
114
PMDD. *See* Premenstrual dysphoric
disorder (PMDD)
PMS, effects of, 62
Postpartum blues, defined, 60

Postpartum depression (PPD)
cause, 61-62
defined, 61, 174
effects of, 61
preventive treatment, 81-82
Postpartum psychosis, defined, 61
Poverty, depression in women
and, 63
PPD. *See* Postpartum depression
(PPD)
Predisposition to depression, 56-57
Pregnancy
lithium and, 142
tricyclic antidepressants (TCAs)
in, 128
Premenstrual dysphoric disorder
(PMDD), defined, 62, 174
Premenstrual syndrome (PMS).
See PMS
Progesterone, side effects, 49
Prozac. *See also* Selective serotonin
reuptake inhibitors (SSRIs)
compliance problems with, 160
incidence of use, 119, 131
personality and, 134-135
Scientology and, 132
side effects, 133-134
Pseudodementia, defined, 32, 174
Psychiatric conditions, effects of,
38-39
Psychiatric nurse specialist,
defined, 85, 174
Psychiatrist, defined, 84-85, 174
Psychoanalysis
defined, 49-50, 91-92, 174
depression and, 92
Psychodynamic therapy. *See also*
Psychotherapy
benefits of, 93
defined, 89, 174
efficacy, 112-113
in children, 114
focus of, 91
length of, 91-92
practitioners, 84

Psychoeducation, defined, 90, 175

Psychologist, defined, 84, 175

Psychomotor agitation
  defined, 12, 175
  depression diagnosis and, 12-13

Psychomotor retardation
  defined, 12, 175
  depression diagnosis and, 12

Psychopharmaceuticals. See
  Psychopharmacology

Psychopharmacology
  defined, 175
  methylphenidate for elderly and,
    137

Psychosis
  defined, 175
  postpartum, defined, 61

Psychosocial, defined, 175

Psychosomatic problems
  defined, 17, 175
  effects of, 17

Psychotherapeutic management.
  See Supportive therapy

Psychotherapy. See also
    Psychodynamic therapy
  clinical depression and, 75
  comparison of types, 112-117
  computer-assisted therapy in, 117
  defined, 175
  feminist, defined, 106-107, 172
  health-care costs and, 116
  licensing, 90
  versus medication, 78, 155-161
  recurrence after, 115, 156-157
  types of, 89

Psychotic depression, defined,
  18, 175

Psychotropics, side effects, 49

Puberty, effects of, 33, 71-72

Q

Quick penalty
  in Rational-Emotive Therapy
    (RET), 105

R

Rapid-cycling phase
  manic-depressive disorder and,
    21, 26, 143
  sleep deprivation and, 154

Rational-emotive therapy (RET),
  defined, 104-105, 175

Reasonable accommodation, The
  1990 Americans With Disabilities
  Act (ADA), 163-166

Recovering memories, 64

Recurrence
  antidepressants and, 124
  psychotherapy and, 115
  psychotherapy versus medication
    and, 155-157
  risk factors, 29-30

Relapse, continuation treatment
  and, 80

Relaxation training, behavioral
  therapy and, 98-99

Retrograde amnesia
  defined, 147, 176
  electroconvulsive therapy (ECT)
    and, 147

Reuptake
  defined, 126, 176
  tricyclic antidepressants (TCAs)
    and, 126

Risk factors, for depression, 29-30

Risk groups, for depression, 31-34

Ritalin. See Methylphenidate

Roll back phenomenon, defined, 79

S

SAD. See Seasonal affective
  disorder (SAD)

Scientology, Prozac and, 132

Seasonal affective disorder (SAD)
  causes, 72-73
  defined, 24, 176
  etiology, 24-25
  incidence, 26

subsyndromal seasonal affective disorder (S-SAD), 25

symptoms, 24-25

treatment, 73, 152-153

Selective serotonin reuptake inhibitors (SSRIs)

for children, 125

combined with light therapy, 152

compliance problems with, 159

defined, 176

mechanism of action, 131

versus tricyclic antidepressants (TCAs), 128

Self-esteem, effects of, 63, 67, 71-72

Self-report scales, 13-14

Senile dementia, misdiagnosis of, 32

Serotonin

antidepressants and, 136

defined, 42, 176

monoamine oxidase inhibitors (MAOIs) and, 129

seasonal affective disorder (SAD) and, 73

tricyclic antidepressants (TCAs) and, 126

Sertaline. *See* Selective serotonin reuptake inhibitors (SSRIs)

Sexual abuse, effects of, 56, 63-64, 71

Sexual appetite, seasonal affective disorder (SAD) and, 24

Shock therapy. *See* Electroconvulsive therapy (ECT)

Signs/symptoms, depression, 12-13

Sleep deprivation, effects of, 154

Sleep disorders

depression diagnosis and, 12

seasonal affective disorder (SAD) and, 24

Sleep EEG. *See* Electroencephalogram (EEG)

Sleep patterns, depression and, 15

Social support, effects of, 55

Social worker, clinical, defined, 84, 170

Soft contact lenses, tricyclic antidepressants (TCAs) and, 128

Steroids

anabolic, side effects, 49

cortisol, 43-44

synthetic, dexamethasone, 43

Stress, effects of, 51-55

Stress Scale, 51-53

Stroke, effects of, 47-48, 77

Styron, William, 37

Subsyndromal seasonal affective disorder (S-SAD), 25

Suicide

bipolar disorder and, 23

cancer pain and, 47

children and, 39-40

depression diagnosis and, 13, 34

elderly and, 39-40

manic-depressive disorder and, 23

panic disorder with depression and, 39

risk of, 39-40

Support groups. *See also* Informational and mutual-aid groups

versus group therapy, 111-112

Supportive therapy, defined, 89-90, 176

Synapse, defined, 42, 176

Syndrome, defined, 12, 176

T

Talk therapy. *See* Psychotherapy

Tamoxifen, antidepressants and, 124

TCAs. *See* Tricyclic antidepressants (TCAs)

Tegretol. *See* Carbamazepine

Television, social effects of, 28-29

Thorazine. *See* Chlorpromazine

Thyroid function, depression and, 15

Thyroid supplements, with antidepressants, 122

Time management, behavioral therapy and, 98-99

Tofranil. *See* Tricyclic antidepressants (TCAs)

Tranylcypromine. *See* Monoamine
oxidase inhibitors (MAOIs)

Trazodone
mechanism of action, 136
side effects, 136

Tremors, antidepressants and, 124

Tricyclic antidepressants (TCAs)
for children, 125
compliance problems with, 159
defined, 176
interactions, 128
mechanism of action, 126
recurrence with, 156-157
versus selective serotonin reuptake
inhibitors (SSRIs), 128
side effects, 126-128

Twain, Mark, manic-depressive
disorder and, 22

Twins
depression in, 44
seasonal affective disorder (SAD)
in, 73

Tylenol, lithium and, 141

Tyramine, and monoamine oxidase
inhibitors (MAOIs), 130

U

Unipolar depression, defined,
15, 176

V

Valproate
lithium alternative, 142-143
side effects, 143

Vegetative, defined, 19, 176

Venlafaxine
mechanism of action, 136
side effects, 136

Victimization, depression in
women and, 63

Vitamin supplements, effects
of, 154

W

Weight loss/gain
depression diagnosis and, 12
seasonal affective disorder (SAD)
and, 24

Winter doldrums, seasonal affective
disorder (SAD) and, 24

Women
depression
biological factors, 60-63
incidence, 25, 31, 33
social/psychological factors,
63-69
dysthymia, incidence, 25
feminist psychotherapy for,
106-107
interpersonal psychotherapy
(IPT) and, 95
manic-depressive disorder and, 46
rapid-cycling phase and, 21, 26
seasonal affective disorder (SAD),
incidence in, 26
stress in, 54
support groups and, 112

Woolf, Virginia, manic-depressive
disorder and, 22

Z

Zoloft. *See* Selective serotonin
reuptake inhibitors (SSRIs)

ZSRDS. *See* Zung Self-Rating
Depression Scale (ZSRDS)

Zung Self-Rating Depression Scale
(ZSRDS), 14